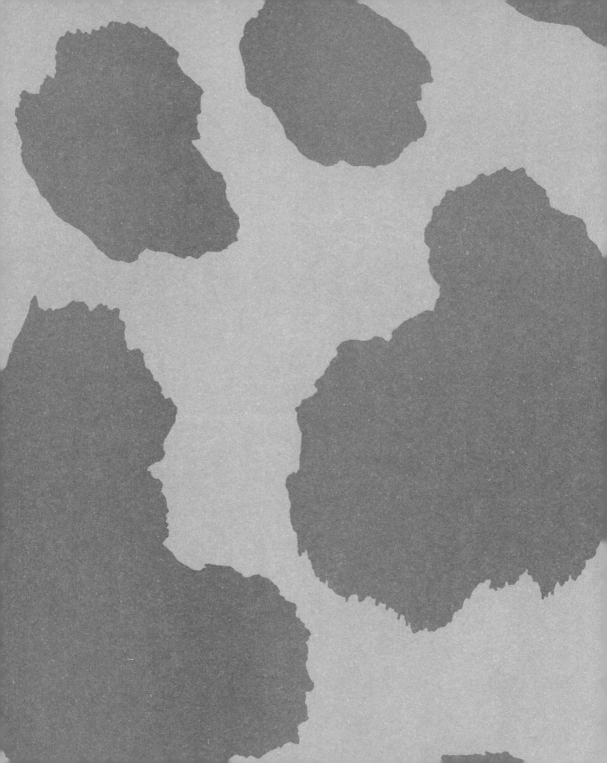

Gerbils

SUE FOX

ANIMAL PLANET ♥ PET CARE LIBRARY

Gerbils

Project Team
Editor: Mary E. Grangeia
Technical Editor: Tom Mazorlig
Copy Editor: Stephanie Fornino
Photo Editor: Heather Russell-Revesz
Interior Design: Leah Lococo Ltd. and Stephanie Krautheim
Design Layout: Stephanie Krautheim

T.F.H. Publications
President/CEO: Glen S. Axelrod
Executive Vice President: Mark E. Johnson
Publisher: Christopher T. Reggio
Production Manager: Kathy Bontz

T.F.H. Publications, Inc.
One TFH Plaza
Third and Union Avenues
Neptune City, NJ 07753

Discovery Communications, Inc. Book Development Team:
Maureen Smith, Executive Vice President & General Manager, Animal Planet
Carol LeBlanc, Vice President, Licensing
Elizabeth Bakacs, Vice President, Creative Services
Peggy Ang, Vice President, Animal Planet Marketing
Caitlin Erb, Licensing Specialist

Printed and bound in China.
06 07 08 09 10 1 3 5 7 9 8 6 4 2

Library of Congress Cataloging-in-Publication Data
Fox, Sue, 1962-
  Gerbils / Sue Fox.
    p. cm. – (Animal planet pet care library)
  Includes index.
  ISBN 978-0-7938-3779-3 (alk. paper)
  1. Gerbils as pets. I. Title.
SF459.G4F692 2007
636.935'83–dc22
                                        2006101387

This book has been published with the intent to provide accurate and authoritative information in regard to the subject matter within. While every precaution has been taken in preparation of this book, the author and publisher expressly disclaim responsibility for any errors, omissions, or adverse effects arising from the use or application of the information contained herein. The techniques and suggestions are used at the reader's discretion and are not to be considered a substitute for veterinary care. If you suspect a medical problem consult your veterinarian.

The Leader in Responsible Animal Care for Over 50 Years!™
www.tfh.com

Table of Contents

Chapter 1

Why I Adore My
Gerbil

Gerbils are ideal small pets. Their cute looks and interesting habits are captivating. Simple to care for, gerbils are usually content to be left alone for long periods of time, such as when their owners are at work or at school. They even can remain unattended in their cage with extra food and water over the weekend.

Very affectionate and lively pets, gerbils quickly learn that their owners represent food and playtime. Their relatively small size makes them easy for children to hold and play with, and they are not intimidating. They will stand up on their hind feet to greet you. However, gerbils are not cuddly pets. Although they like to be petted, they also like to bounce around and play rather than being held for long periods of time.

Natural History

Although they are now kept as pets all over the world, Mongolian gerbils began life in captivity as laboratory animals. During the early 1900s, many scientists and medical researchers were interested in obtaining new species of rodent for use in scientific studies. These previously unknown rodents were susceptible to some of the same diseases that people get, and by studying them, scientists could learn how to more effectively treat these illnesses.

In 1935, a Japanese scientist caught twenty pairs of Mongolian gerbils from the Amur River basin located on the border of China and Russia. The gerbils readily bred in captivity and proved useful in the laboratory. In 1954, four breeding pairs were sent from Japan to the United States. Twenty-four breeding pairs were sent to Great Britain in 1964 by the United States. In such a fashion, laboratory colonies of Mongolian gerbils were established in various countries around the world. Scientists gave them special notice because they were naturally gentle and not likely to bite.

Gerbils first became available as pets in North America in 1964. Since then, their inquisitive nature, calm demeanor, and clean habits have made them a popular pet. Gerbils are cute, easy to care for, and practically odorless. Even though they are lively and agile, they are also docile. Unlike other small pets, such as hamsters, gerbils are not timid and nervous. Brave and curious, they will eagerly explore your hand or anything else put near them. Instead of running away from something unknown, an alert and

Gerbils stand on their hind feet to greet their owners.

Gerbils have been bred in captivity for more than 70 years.

inquisitive gerbil will often advance and investigate.

Domesticated Gerbils

Gerbils have been bred in captivity for more than 70 years. During that time, they changed in many ways compared to their wild ancestors. In 1995, scientists on an expedition to central Mongolia captured wild gerbils for their research. When comparing the wild gerbils and their offspring to laboratory gerbils, the scientists discovered many interesting differences.

From the outside, few obvious changes were apparent. The wild gerbils tended to be smaller than their tame counterparts—their body and tail length were shorter, and they weighed less. But more interestingly, scientists found that the tame gerbils learned differently and had brains that weighed less. The scientists noted that the seizures sometimes seen in tame gerbils did not occur in the wild gerbils and were rare in their offspring. Also, in their native habitat, wild gerbils breed from February to October. However, tame gerbils are not dependent on day length and can breed throughout the year. Moreover, the average number of babies born to tame gerbils is greater than the number born to wild ones. These changes in physiology, behavior, and reproduction have convinced many scientists that the gerbils bred in captivity for the past 70 years are now truly domesticated.

Gerbils in Experiments

Scientists first became interested in using gerbils in research because they are susceptible to Tyzzer's disease (see page 79). This bacterial disease commonly affects young animals, including puppies, kittens, calves, and foals, and it can be deadly. Gerbils also are used in a variety of other scientific investigations, including behavioral studies and research on parasitism, neurology, and hearing. Like people, gerbils can experience strokes, so scientists have used them in numerous studies. They also are important models for aging and epilepsy. The information that scientists gain from them has improved the lives of people and other animals as well as the lives of other gerbils.

Scientific Names

Scientific names are the means by which scientists from all over the world refer to the same species of animal. The reason that scientific names are used is that an animal can have several different common names. Common names can vary by region and can even be the same as another animal's common name. For example, the Mongolian gerbil is also known by the names of Mongolian desert gerbil, clawed gerbil, and clawed jird. But its scientific name, *Meriones unguiculatus,* is always the same. The only way to know for certain which species you are reading about is by the scientific name.

A species name is made of two parts, the genus and the species epithet. Hence, the Mongolian gerbil belongs to the genus *Meriones,* and its unique species name is *unguiculatus.* The genus and species names are always italicized or underlined. To differentiate the domesticated gerbils from wild gerbils, some scientists have proposed that domesticated gerbils should be called *Meriones unguiculatus forma domestica.* You might see the gerbil's scientific name cited as *Meriones unguiculatus* Milne-Edwards, 1867. The last name of the individual who officially described the gerbil for the first time in a publication and the year of the publication are attached to the gerbil's scientific name. Thus, Alphonse Milne-Edwards is the researcher who officially named the Mongolian gerbil in 1867.

The gerbil didn't get his modern scientific name until 1908. *Meriones* is Greek for warrior, while *unguiculatus* is Latin for "with claws." Thus, the

The Expert Knows

Life Span

Gerbils live two to four years, but some occasionally live to be five years old. Make sure that once the novelty of owning gerbils wears off, you will still be interested in caring for your pets. Unenthusiastically caring for them, or worse, neglecting them, is not fair. Consider whether you will still be interested in caring for these pets one, two, or four years from now.

gerbil's name translates into "warrior with claws." This is a fierce-sounding name for such a small furry creature and perhaps not entirely appropriate. While Mongolian gerbils vigorously defend their territory against other gerbils, they don't use their claws as much as they use their teeth.

Gerbil Relatives

There are at least 80 known species of gerbil. Most live in arid climates in desert habitats. They are found in desert areas throughout Africa, parts of Europe, and across Asia into China. Sometimes other species of gerbil are offered for sale by pet stores. These include the fat-tailed duprasi (*Pachyuromys duprasi*), pallid gerbil (*Gerbillus perpallidus*), Persian jird (*Meriones persicus*), and Shaw's jird (*Meriones shawi*). Some of these species are smaller than the Mongolian gerbil, while a few are larger. Do not house different species together, because they are likely to fight. The housing requirement for most species of gerbil is the same; larger species should be provided with a correspondingly larger cage. However, dietary requirements can vary. In some cases, live foods such as mealworms must be regularly offered. Additional information on species requirements can be found on websites devoted to gerbils and their care. If you know the species' scientific name, the library is also a good source of information on diet. Ideally, the pet store employee or breeder should be able to alert you to any differences in care from that needed by the Mongolian gerbil.

In the Wild

Mongolian gerbils are native to the cold desert and semi-arid grasslands of Mongolia and northeastern China.

Very hot summers and very cold winters are typical of their natural habitat. Gerbils are well adapted to the extreme temperature fluctuations between day and night and between winter and summer. Adaptations such as living in an underground network of burrows, foraging for food both at night and during the day, storing food, and deriving water metabolically from the foods they eat help them survive in the arid environment.

Wild gerbils are colored so that they blend into their desert habitat. The dense fur on their back is a golden sandy color, and the fur on their belly is pale gray or off-white. Like a kangaroo, gerbils have long, muscular hind legs that enable them to hop and leap quickly. Their front legs are shorter and are used to hold food and to dig. Unlike rodents such as rats and mice, they have blocky, not pointed, muzzles.

Gerbils measure about 9 inches (22.8 cm) in length, including their long, fur-covered tail, which helps them keep their balance when they sit up and aids them in leaping and turning when pursued by a predator. If a gerbil is grabbed by the black tuft at the tip of his tail, he will lose the skin, exposing the vertebrae, and the tuft will not regrow. A variety of animals prey on wild gerbils, including weasels, snakes, and owls.

The Burrow

To dig a burrow, a gerbil uses his front feet to rapidly excavate dirt. With his hind feet, he kicks the dirt out of the enlarging tunnel. The burrow can extend underground to a depth of about 2 feet (0.6 m). This depth helps to moderate the temperatures so that the burrow stays relatively cool when it is hot above ground and warm when it

Including their tail, gerbils measure about 9 inches (22.8 cm) in length.

is cold above ground. Gerbils maintain a tidy orderliness in their elaborate burrow system. Besides multiple entrances, they have separate nesting chambers, food storage rooms, and bathroom areas. A gerbil's long whiskers help him navigate his dark underground tunnels, which can extend over 25 feet (25.6 m) in length.

Physical Characteristics

Sight and Sound
Gerbils have large eyes that help them see when foraging at night. Unlike people, they have a wide field of vision because their eyes are on the sides of their head. When a gerbil sees an unexpected movement, especially overhead, he doesn't wait to figure out what made it; instead, he immediately flees into a burrow. Gerbils do not rely on their vision as much as they do on their other senses. Even though their ears are small, they have acute hearing. They readily can hear low-frequency sounds that people cannot detect. The ability to do so can help them evade predators because they can hear the low-frequency sounds made by the wings of a predator such as an owl.

Hoarding Food
Although their population can fluctuate in response to food shortages, gerbils are a relatively common rodent in most of their native habitat. In the summer, they

Gerbils communicate with each other by squeaking.

are active during the day and the night. But in winter, they only come above ground on sunny days. Because they do not hibernate, they need a source of food in winter. Female and male gerbils of all ages collect food and store it in underground chambers during autumn. Then in winter, each family group eats the stored food. Besides collecting plants, seeds, and grains from the wild parts of their habitat, they also collect

Gerbils and the Law

In some states, certain species of pets are not legal for pet stores to sell or for you to own. Although there is national legislation that governs the keeping of animals, individual states still have their own laws, and these laws vary from state to state, from county to county, and even from city to city. States can ban personal ownership of an animal species for various reasons. For example, in California, one of the most restrictive states, it is not legal to keep gerbils as pets. Certain species of animal can be listed as prohibited to prevent depletion of wild populations and to provide for animal welfare, or because they pose a threat to native wildlife, agricultural interests, or public health and safety. The California Department of Fish and Game has banned gerbils because of concerns that if they become established in the wild, they could damage crops and displace native wildlife.

seeds and grains from farmers' fields. One researcher found more than 3.3 pounds (1.5 kg) of grain in one gerbil storeroom!

Smell and Scent Glands

Gerbils are not noisy little animals. They don't seem to communicate with each other using their voice as much as they rely on scent. Both males and females have a scent gland on their belly. The gland is not conspicuous; it looks like a small hairless area in the middle of their belly. The gland produces a yellow-brown musty-smelling secretion, but the scent is most obvious to other gerbils, so you are unlikely to notice it. By sniffing each other's belly, these animals can tell familiar from unfamiliar gerbils and whether an individual is a male or female. They mark items in their cage with their scent by pressing their belly against each item as they walk over it. They also mark other gerbils with their scent. When one gerbil mounts another of the same sex, he or she is actually marking the other gerbil, not mating. Dominant gerbils mark more than subordinate individuals. Gerbils also communicate with each other by means of their urine and piles of droppings, which they also use to mark their territories.

Behavior

Mongolian gerbils are social rodents who live in family groups. Each burrow system is inhabited by a pair of adults and their offspring of various ages. Only one female in a group that shares a burrow will have babies. The older youngsters do not breed but instead help their parents rear their younger siblings. They will remain in their parents' burrow during their first winter. The adult male also helps to care for the babies by snuggling with them, defending the territory, collecting nesting material, and hoarding food. Gerbils are mostly monogamous, but both the male and female will sometimes mate with gerbils outside their territories. This helps to prevent inbreeding. Until they leave their parents' burrow, the young gerbils will not be able to reproduce. Many believe that the adults suppress their sexual development.

Gerbils are territorial and will chase and attack an unfamiliar individual who tries to enter their territory. The home range for the Mongolian gerbil can encompass almost 1/2 of a mile (0.8-1.6 km). The need for a large home range is probably due to the desert environment in which they live; gerbils probably need to forage long distances to find sufficient food.

Gerbil Talk

Gerbils have many interesting behaviors. They communicate with each other by squeaking and by thumping their back legs during courtship, playing, and when alarmed. In the wild, they use their hind feet to drum on the ground and warn each other of approaching danger. Friendly behavior among gerbils includes sniffing noses or mouths and nudging their head beneath each other's rump. Family members also groom each other. Gerbils make ultrasonic

Dedicated hobbyists breed specifically for a docile temperament.

14

sounds, presumably as a means of communicating with each other.

The Harderian Gland

The Harderian gland performs several functions. It is located behind a gerbil's eyes and secretes a reddish fluid that keeps the eyes moist. The fluid then drains into the outer part of the nose through the nasolacrimal duct. When a gerbil grooms himself, he spreads the Harderian gland fluid over his body. This fluid is the main source of oils found on his fur. When it is cold out, a gerbil increases the amount of time he spends grooming himself. This increases the amount of insulating oils on his coat, which protects him against the cold temperature. When temperatures become warmer, he removes the insulating oils by rolling in sand. If a gerbil is not allowed to sand bathe, the excess oils can accumulate in the coat, making it matted and oily. Research also has suggested that the Harderian gland fluid influences a

female's willingness to breed. Hence, gerbils sniff each other's faces to gain information, presumably conveyed by the Harderian gland fluid.

Where to Buy Your Gerbil

Before you buy your gerbil, purchase a cage and supplies and have everything ready prior to bringing him home. A clean pet store is a good place to buy them. Other options include humane societies, friends who breed gerbils, or hobbyists who are members of gerbil clubs. Gerbils who are bred in large numbers are sometimes less friendly than those bred by hobbyists specifically selecting for a docile temperament.

Although you might find it surprising, gerbils are exhibited in shows just like dogs, cats, and horses. They are judged by experts who determine how closely they conform to the ideal standard for shape, appearance, and color or markings for their variety.

Of most importance to potential pet owners, show gerbils must be docile and easy to handle. Those who are nervous, timid, or who try to bite are less likely to win awards. Hobbyists who show their gerbils preferably breed individuals who have won awards; thus, any with undesirable temperaments are less likely to be bred. Because temperament has a hereditary component, show gerbils bred by hobbyists tend to have better pet qualities (for example, they are confident, not nervous) than randomly obtained ones whose heredity is unknown. You can find hobbyists who breed gerbils in the advertisement section of pet magazines and Internet sites devoted to these pets.

Female or Male?

Some experienced gerbil keepers think that females are more active and curious than males, and that males are calmer than females. However, not all hobbyists agree with this generalization. Male gerbils are larger than females and have a somewhat stronger odor because of their scent secretions. Unless their cage is not regularly cleaned, people cannot readily detect the odor.

Young male gerbils can be differentiated from females by their dark-colored scrotum located near the base of the tail. This difference is easier to detect in adults. Because you are preferably buying young gerbils, you must determine their gender by comparing them to their cagemates. The distance between the anus and the genital papilla will be much greater in the male than in the female. You also might notice a slight swelling

Gerbil Development

Gestation period	25–28 days
Gestation period*	Up to 42 days
Litter size	4–6
Ears open	3–7 days
Hair/coat grows	7–10 days
Incisors erupt	12–14 days
Eyes open	14–20 days
First crawl out of nest	10 days
Weaning	21–28 days
Estrous period	4–6 days
Length of female fertility	18 months
Length of male fertility	24 months

* The gestation period is lengthened if the female is nursing a litter.

> *Domestic gerbils come in almost two dozen colors.*

where the male's scrotum is located. The female also has nipples, but these can be difficult to see. Blowing on the gerbil's belly can part the hair enough to detect the nipples. Pet store employees should be able to help you determine the gender of your pets.

Be aware that a female might be pregnant if she was not separated soon enough from the males. Gerbils can first breed between 9 and 12 weeks of age. Baby gerbils, called pups, are born pink and hairless with their eyes closed after a gestation period of 25 to 28 days. Usually, 4 to 6 babies are born in a litter, but as many as 12 in one litter have been reported. Because of this possibility, try to buy your gerbils from a pet store where the females are kept separate from the males. If this is not possible, check to see whether the pet store employees

> *A young gerbil will be easier to tame and handle.*

know how old they are; the answer will help you determine the likelihood of a female being pregnant.

How Many?

Gerbils should be kept in pairs. A gerbil kept by himself will be unhappy and will not thrive. If you decide to keep a male and female gerbil together, you can expect your pets to constantly have babies. While this can be fun and interesting, consider whether you will be able to find new homes for all the babies your pets will be making. A pair of gerbils can produce a new litter of babies every 30 to 40 days for a total of six to seven litters over the female's reproductive life, which is about one-and-a-half years. Pet stores might be interested, but they might not always need gerbils when you are trying to find new homes for your weaned youngsters. If you are going to breed gerbils, consider choosing ones with the less common colors, because pet stores are often more interested in such varieties.

If you don't want to breed gerbils, either purchase two females or purchase two males. Opinions differ as to whether two males get along better than two females. Some hobbyists report that males tend to fight as they get older, but others think that females tend to become ornerier with each other. Because there is no agreement, choose whichever gender you prefer. Alternatively, a qualified veterinarian can spay a female or neuter a male, which would eliminate the gerbil's ability to breed. (Although altering

Showing Gerbils

Gerbils are exhibited in shows throughout the world. Showing is a fun way to meet other people who also like gerbils. At a show, you can learn the latest information regarding their care and also find out about the development of new colors. In showing, gerbils are usually divided into different categories based on their color. The national gerbil society of each country develops the standards for each color type, and these societies are in charge of the criteria that judges use to evaluate them. Gerbils are judged on similar factors as other show animals—for example, conformation (body type), color, coat, and health. An animal can be penalized for various faults, such as dirty or stained fur, and can be disqualified if he has a nasty temperament. Information on getting started showing gerbils can be obtained by contacting your national gerbil society.

rabbits and ferrets is a fairly common procedure, it is rarely performed on gerbils.)

Buy two young gerbils at the same time so that they can grow up together. Adults (about 12 weeks old) are territorial and will fight if another gerbil is introduced into their home. A pair will form a lifelong bond. They

Gerbils and Children

Very young children always need to be watched when they are playing with pets. If a gerbil struggles while being held, some children tend to squeeze even harder instead of relaxing their hold. Sometimes this rough handling can frighten a gerbil and cause him to bite. The child might then drop or throw him, which can be fatal. A parent can help reduce the risk of a bite by showing children how to properly hold their pet and by instructing them on what to do should he begin to wiggle—for example, when returning the gerbil into his cage.

Children also should be told to open the cage and let their gerbils come to them rather than pulling them out of their home. If they are sleeping, children should call their pets' names, allowing them to stretch, yawn, and slowly wake up. However, if the gerbils curl back into sleeping balls, the children need to wait until later to visit with them.

If gerbils will be in a child's care, make sure that the child chooses them. Children who select their own pets feel more responsibility for and attachment to them.

will wrestle and play-fight together, taking turns chasing each other around their cage. The two gerbils also will groom each other and curl up to sleep together. Keeping more than two together in the same cage is not recommended, because a third gerbil is likely to be bullied by the other two.

Varieties

Throughout the world, all the gerbils kept as pets and laboratory animals descend from the original 20 gerbils who were caught in 1935. Domestic gerbils went through another "genetic bottleneck" in 1954 when only four breeding pairs gave rise to all those found in the United States and Europe. Domestic varieties have low genetic variation because of these bottlenecks. Despite the small number of "founder" gerbils, both laboratory and pet gerbils thrive and have given rise to considerable variation. Of most interest to pet owners are the different colors in which they are now found.

All small animals kept in captivity, including gerbils, rats, mice, rabbits, and guinea pigs, eventually develop mutations from their normal color. Such mutations are rare. In the wild, animals that are unusual in color are more noticeable to predators and often do not live long enough to reproduce. Hence, unusual colors are not typically found in wild populations. A conspicuous color is not a problem for pet animals, because people protect pets from potential predators. Hobbyists have increased the prevalence of color mutations by selectively breeding gerbils with desirable colors.

In the wild, gerbils come in only one color, agouti, but domestic gerbils come in almost two dozen colors. The most common colors include agouti and black, followed by argente (orange), ruby-eyed white, lilac (deep gray), dove (light gray), and nutmeg (mix of brown, black, and orange). Other attractive but rare colors include Himalayan and Siamese. Just like with cats, the tail, feet, ears, and nose are darker colors than the rest of the body. You are most likely to obtain uncommon and rare colors, such as honey cream and Burmese, from breeders rather than from pet stores. However, many interesting colors, such as the Burmese, first got started when an intrepid gerbil breeder found the unusual-colored animals in a pet store.

Gerbils also come in what are known as "marked colors," which means that they

Let your new gerbil get used to his surroundings.

have one or more patches of color on a solid background. The patches can be spots on prescribed areas, such as the nose and forehead, or pied, which is a background color broken by patches of white, usually with a white shawl around the shoulders. Mutations in coat length and texture have not yet appeared, although they might develop in the future.

A gerbil's eye color is black, red, or pink. The latter color is only found in white gerbils.

Pet stores usually do not stock a wide variety of gerbils. If you want a particular color, ask whether the store can special order one for you from their suppliers. Alternatively, check gerbil websites, because breeders often have a greater variety of different-colored animals for sale.

By learning about genetics and carefully keeping track of the results of each pairing, breeders are able to develop new color mutations. The genetics of coat colors and markings are well known, which means that experienced breeders know what color the babies will be from particular pairings.

Breeders attempt to "fix" the desirable trait by line breeding—for example, breeding a father with a daughter or a brother to a sister. Due to inbreeding, line breeding can sometimes cause problems such as a shorter life span, greater susceptibility to health problems, or reduced fertility. Should you ever choose to show gerbils, you eventually must learn more about the inheritance of color. You could even try to develop a new color variety.

Some hobbyists think that gerbils of a certain color or coat pattern are gentler and calmer when compared to other varieties. While some individuals

Healthy gerbils are active and curious.

Nervous at First

When you first bring your gerbils home, they might be frightened or nervous. Let them settle down and get used to their new environment before you play with them. Use this time to think of names for your pets to help you tame them. They will learn to associate their names with feeding and playtime. In many cases, gerbils are immediately comfortable in their new surroundings and will respond well to your friendly attempts. You can offer them some of their food in your hand, but if they seem shy and nervous, leave them alone for a while, or talk soothingly to them. Sometimes partially covering all but the front of their cage with a brown paper bag will help them feel more secure and less vulnerable because they will be able to detect less motion around their enclosure. Don't use a towel over a wire frame cage because your gerbils will pull it into their cage and gnaw holes in it.

of a certain variety might have these desirable traits, unfortunately, there are currently too many exceptions to state with any confidence that one variety makes a better pet than another.

How Old?

Pick a young gerbil because he will be much easier to tame and will make a better pet than an older one who has been infrequently handled. A young gerbil also will live longer than an older animal. Gerbils are weaned between three and four weeks of age and are ready to go to their new homes between four and eight weeks of age or when about 2 to 3 inches (5.1-7.6 cm) in body length. However, do not buy a baby who was just weaned. Weaning, as well as going to a new home, are stressful events that can cause a baby gerbil to get sick. A slightly older gerbil will be hardier and just as cute. If necessary, you can estimate a gerbil's age by comparing his body length to the adult size.

You also want to choose gerbils ten weeks of age or younger because at that age it is easier to pair new, unfamiliar gerbils together. If you have to buy older individuals, you need to purchase them from the same cage so that they already know each other, or you might need to use the split-cage method to house them in the same cage.

Choosing Healthy Gerbils

The premises of the pet store or breeder from which you buy your pets should be clean, with minimal odor. While some smell is normal, if the odor in the store or from the cage is excessively pungent, buy your gerbils from another pet store. Check to be

Choose a gerbil who has sleek, shiny fur and clear, bright eyes.

sure that they have food and water. An empty food dish or water bottle is a sign of poor care, and the gerbils are less likely to be healthy.

Choose your pets from a clean, uncrowded cage. Gerbils who come from a dirty, crowded environment are less likely to be healthy. No matter how much you might like a particular gerbil or want to buy your pets immediately, do not buy one if any of the gerbils in a cage exhibit symptoms of ill health. Although the ones you want might appear healthy, they have been exposed to sick animals and are likely to become ill at a later time, often from the stress of going to a new home.

A healthy gerbil should have dense, shiny fur. The coat should be smooth and sleek, with no bald areas or flaky skin. The eyes should be clear and bright. Your choice should look solid and a little plump, not frail. Do not choose a gerbil who is listless, sneezes, has runny eyes or a runny nose, a rough or thin coat, lumps, or scabs. Dirty, matted fur near the tail could be a sign of diarrhea. Because sick gerbils wipe their nose on the inside of their front feet, check to be sure that the fur in these areas is not wet or matted, which would indicate illness. If possible, ask the pet store employee or breeder to help you check that the front teeth are properly aligned.

Healthy gerbils are active and curious. If they are sleeping, they should wake up and investigate when their cage is opened. They should not limp or move awkwardly. If a gerbil is missing part of his tail, it could be because of improper care, or his tail might have gotten caught in an exercise wheel. A kinked tail is thought to be inherited and is considered a fault in a show animal. However, a gerbil with a damaged tail will still make a good pet and live a long, healthy life. Carefully scrutinize the animal and his surroundings to make sure that nothing else is awry.

Personality

If possible, spend some time looking at the gerbils available from various pet stores and breeders. Handling them or watching a pet store employee or breeder do so will give you an idea of their temperament. A gerbil's temperament or personality is important to the quality of your pet-owning experience.

Gerbils range in personality from calm and friendly to somewhat skittish. Most pet owners enjoy a calm pet better than they do a skittish one. Personality is affected by breeding (heredity) and the environment in which gerbils are reared. While it is not possible for you to assess family background, the environment that you provide and how often you play with them will affect their personality. By providing quality care and slowly taming your gerbils, you are more likely to end up with enjoyable pets.

You can increase the likelihood that you are buying pets with good personalities by choosing individuals who are inquisitive and who investigate your hand when you place them in the cage. A good choice is one who is bold and curious and climbs onto your hand when you place him in the cage. A gerbil who sniffs your hand, runs away, but returns to further investigate is also a good choice. Just like puppies, some gerbils will explore their environment by nipping with their teeth. A nip from a gerbil is not painful. It might startle you or frighten a child, but it will not draw blood. Do not choose a gerbil who runs and hides, is aggressive and tries to bite, or who struggles frantically when held.

Coming Home

After selecting your gerbils, be sure to ask the pet store employee to show you how to properly hold them. It is important that you are comfortable handling your pets before you leave the store. Ask the pet store employee to place a small handful of shavings from the cage into the box that you are using to transport them. Place the old shavings into your pets' new home. The familiar smell can help them settle more comfortably into their environment. If your new pets' home is not yet set up for their occupancy, have someone else watch them while you arrange their quarters. Gerbils can quickly chew their way out of the cardboard box provided by pet stores for the trip to your home.

The Stuff of

Everyday Life

Before you bring your gerbils home, you'll need to have a few items on hand to make them feel safe and comfortable when they arrive in their new and unfamiliar environment. These will include housing, bedding, food dishes, water bottles, some toys, and basic grooming supplies.

Housing

You can find suitable housing for your gerbils at a pet store. A cage is the most expensive piece of equipment that you will need to buy. The general rule when buying a cage is to choose the largest one that you can afford. Gerbils are very active animals and need a roomy home. A cage that is too small and confining will become dirty and smelly more quickly, and it can lead to fights among your pets, who will become irritable without enough space. The more space you provide your gerbils in which to play and explore, the more interesting and healthy they will be. The enclosure you choose should be large enough to allow them room for separate eating, sleeping, and toilet areas, as well as one or two exercise wheels.

Cages are available in many shapes, sizes, and styles. Gerbils can be housed in glass aquariums, wire frame cages, or combination cages made of wire and plastic. Regardless of what style you choose, a few general rules apply. Gerbils are not arboreal (living in trees). Although they might occasionally climb into shrubs to forage on leaves and bark in their native habitat, they are not acrobatic climbers like pet rats. Being ground dwellers, they do best in a cage that provides plenty of floor space rather than in a tall one with room to climb. However, most manufacturers design their cages with extra vertical space in two or three

A 10-gallon (37.9 l) glass aquarium will provide a good home for a pair of gerbils.

stories. Luckily, gerbils are adaptable; if possible, though, choose a single-level enclosure with abundant floor space.

Being able to easily reach into the cage to perform daily tasks such as cleaning and providing fresh food will help to make these chores much easier. Whether it has both a top and front door or one large front door, at least one should be large enough for you to comfortably reach all areas within the cage and enable you to easily remove a gerbil in your hand. Each door should latch securely and not be easily pushed out at a corner by a persistent pet. No matter what type of housing you buy, immediately replace any part of it that is chewed or damaged because it will not take long for your gerbils to find the damaged area and escape.

Aquariums

A 10-gallon (37.9 l) glass aquarium with a secure wire-screen cover will provide a good home for a pair of gerbils. Because resourceful gerbils always can find a way out, their cage always must be covered. Pet stores sell wire screens with latches to secure the top to the aquarium just for this purpose. The latches are a necessity because these small animals can easily push a screen up just enough to slip out beneath it. Books and bricks placed on top as extra weight might be necessary, but extra latches are probably more secure. As an added benefit, you can easily reach your pets because the entire top lifts off the enclosure.

As is their nature, gerbils spend a lot of time digging and kicking shavings and food about their cage. Compared to a wire frame cage, an aquarium will keep the area around your pets' home tidy because debris cannot spill out of the enclosure. However, the glass sides can become dirty and difficult to see through if they are not kept clean.

Because there are no wire bars, gerbils are unlikely to injure their noses by gnawing on them.

If you choose a glass aquarium with a simple lid, keep in mind that this type of housing is not as well ventilated as a wire cage. While aquariums are beneficial because they are not drafty, poor ventilation and lax cleaning habits can cause ammonia gas to build up to uncomfortable levels. This can irritate the respiratory system. For your pets' health, you must be vigilant in keeping such housing clean. An alternative to the simple lid is the double- and triple-story tank topper made to fit securely over a glass aquarium. This option provides your pets with the best of both worlds— extra space with ventilation. Keep in mind that aquariums are heavier than wire cages and can be more difficult for a child to move and clean.

Wire frame cages have good ventilation.

Wire Frame Cages

A wire cage that measures 20 inches (50.8 cm) long by 12 inches (30.5 cm) wide by 10 inches (25.4 cm) high will provide a good home for a pair of gerbils. Wire frame cages made of galvanized steel have good ventilation and offer a good view of your pets. A good-quality one should be easy to clean with a slide-out or snap-off bottom tray. The plastic trays of some cages are attractively colored and can be color coordinated to match a room's décor. The wire

frame should prevent your gerbils from reaching the plastic tray; they are prolific chewers and will readily gnaw on it.

As with all enclosures, the wire cage should have a large door opening that allows you to easily reach inside and take your gerbil out. Check that the door latches securely and cannot be easily pushed out at a corner by your pets. The one that you select shouldn't have any sharp metal edges. The best styles will have both a door and a removable top or side to provide easy access to the interior of the enclosure. A cage handle can make moving it easier. No matter what, the wire mesh that composes the body of the cage should feel strong and durable, not soft and flimsy.

Most manufacturers label these cages for specific kinds of small pets, such as for rabbits, gerbils, or hamsters. The labeling usually provides reasonable guidelines. You can generally rely upon the information supplied as to the right size to purchase for your particular pet. If you have any doubts, always err in favor of choosing a larger

cage rather than a smaller one. Gerbils can sometimes use the larger cages designed for hamsters and mice. However, because they must be kept in pairs, whereas hamsters can be kept singly, not all hamster cages provide adequate space. The bar spacing should measure no more than ½ an inch (1.27 cm) apart to prevent young gerbils from squeezing between the bars and escaping.

If you buy a wire cage with vertical bars that measure more than ½ inch (1.27 cm) apart, such as a cage made for rabbits or guinea pigs, you will need to modify it. Attach a heavy-gauge wire mesh (not window screen!) that measures no greater than ¼ inch (0.64 cm) square to the outside using metal clips. Do not use plastic ties, lightweight wire, or string to attach the additional wire mesh. These materials are not durable enough to withstand a gerbil's chewing. The wire mesh should attach tightly to the original bars to prevent your pets from squeezing between the two layers of wire and accidentally getting stuck. Metal cages do have some other drawbacks. While they provide good ventilation, they are also potentially drafty. Over time, a gerbil's relatively concentrated urine can corrode the metal pan

Catching a Lost Gerbil

Despite all your precautions, your gerbil might escape from his home or run away while you are playing with him. An escape is hazardous to your pet's health; he can starve to death or be eaten by other household pets such as dogs, cats, ferrets, and pet rats. An escaped gerbil also can be very destructive, chewing on furniture, walls, and electrical wires. If your pet escapes outside, your chances of finding him alive again are not good. In the ideal situation, your gerbil is still in your house and you know which room he might be in. First try to find him by conducting a thorough search of every room. Once a room is cleared, place books along the door margin to prevent him from squeezing underneath. Have your pet's nest box and some tasty treats, such as sunflower seeds, with you while you conduct your search. If you see your gerbil, don't make any quick moves toward him because doing so will frighten him and cause him to run away.

Move slowly, talk gently, and try to get close enough to offer him a sunflower seed. Alternatively, place his nest box close to where you saw him and trail some bedding and sunflower seeds into the entry; your gerbil might just dash for his "bedroom."

If these techniques do not work, place your pet's cage on the floor next to a wall in the blocked-off room where you think he is loose. Leave a trail of sunflower seeds to the cage. Do not leave the cage door open because your other gerbil will probably join the wanderer. Instead, provide that gerbil with a new nest box. Take the old nest box, along with the nesting material and fresh food, and place it on the floor outside and next to the cage. Sometimes the escaped gerbil will return to the cage area and then fall asleep inside his familiar nest box.

However, if your pet has decided some secret location makes a better place to sleep and hoard sunflower seeds, you must trap him. You can use a variety of other methods to catch an escaped gerbil, including a ramp and empty bucket baited with irresistible food, such as sunflower seeds. When he walks up the ramp, he'll fall into the bucket. However, the most effective and simple method is a harmless have-a-heart live trap baited with rolled oats and peanut butter. These traps are readily purchased at hardware stores or large chain stores. Place the live trap on the floor adjacent to a wall. Using more than one trap increases your chances of quickly recapturing your pet. Buy traps made for mice, not the larger rat-sized traps.

that fits beneath them. You can help to prevent this problem by cleaning your pets' bathroom area every few days or by lining the tray bottom with newspaper (as long as your gerbils do not have access to the tray). Plastic trays will not corrode from urine.

Gerbils have small feet that can accidentally become caught and twisted in the wire floor of a metal cage. If the one you choose has a wire rather than a solid floor, you must be certain to completely cover the floor with bedding to prevent this potential problem. Doing so will also prevent food stores from dropping through the wire screen where they cannot be reached.

If you choose a wire frame cage, try to find one with high-bottom tray sides to catch bedding and other debris that will be kicked out during normal daily activities. Alternatively, place the housing on top of newspaper that extends for several inches (cms) more than the diameter of the bottom surface, or place the cage inside a kitty litter pan to catch the material

that spills out. You can also purchase a cloth seed guard sold in the bird section of a pet store, which works nicely.

Combination Wire and Plastic Cages

Combination cages constructed of wire screen and hard plastic are made for both gerbils and hamsters. These brightly colored cages are a lot of fun because the connecting tubes allow you to expand your pets' cage into a playground. However, be picky with this type of housing, because some models can provide even less ventilation than aquariums. The enclosure and tubes quickly become smelly if they are not cleaned frequently. Some gerbils even gnaw through the plastic tubes and escape. The plastic must be regularly washed. Over time, your pets' nails will scratch the plastic parts and can make them difficult to see through. In response to these drawbacks, many manufacturers have redesigned them to provide much better ventilation and ease in cleaning. If you want a combination cage for your gerbils, be sure to select a model with maximum ventilation. Before buying, check that the door is large enough for you to reach in and easily take out your pets.

Unsuitable Cages

Gerbils are experts at escaping their enclosures. This means that the cage you choose must be well constructed and escape proof. A wooden enclosure is not recommended. Using their strong sharp teeth and powerful jaw muscles, your gerbils will quickly chew their way out. Because wood absorbs urine and other odors, these habitats also are difficult to keep clean.

Unless they are the same size as a 10-gallon (37.9 l) aquarium, the rectangular plastic enclosures with snap-on lids, sometimes called small animal habitats, are not typically large enough to house a pair of gerbils. They make suitable carrying cages to take your new pets

Gerbilariums

Providing your gerbils with a dirt gerbilarium is fun and allows you to observe their more natural behaviors. Use either a 10- or 20-gallon (37.9-75.7 l) aquarium covered with a flat lid, or use a multi-story topper cage. Fill half of the aquarium with dirt. You can use soil sold at a garden supply store. Don't buy soil with amendments such as plant food, and avoid potting soil because it lacks clay and is so fine that it cannot hold a burrow's shape without collapsing onto the gerbils. Pack the dirt into the aquarium. You need to keep the soil somewhat moist but not damp so that your gerbils' tunnels will not collapse. An alternative to dirt is a deep mix of shavings and hay in which your pets can construct tunnels.

For some greenery, sprout seeds from your gerbils' food. Let the plants grow several inches (cm) tall and develop a strong root system in a pot before you transfer them to the aquarium. Your gerbils will eat and root around the plants. If you place a rock in the aquarium, you might notice that your gerbils mark it with both their scent gland and their droppings. Try adding a low branch for them to climb on and mark.

You can partially bury some plastic tubes or cardboard toilet paper rolls for use as "starter burrows." Until your gerbils have excavated some tunnels, provide them with a nest box and a large supply of soft nesting material. Don't forget a water bottle.

A gerbilarium presents some problems. If your gerbils have established an underground bathroom, you will not be able to clean their cage easily. Some will dig up dirty nesting material and bring it to the surface, at which time you can remove it. However, when it is time to clean the enclosure, all the dirt must be discarded. Some keepers note that their pets become more "wild" and less tame when they are kept in a gerbilarium.

Shavings made from hardwoods are best for gerbils.

home or to the veterinarian, and they provide a secure place to keep them while you are cleaning their cage, but they should not be a permanent home. Be careful with these cages because if you drop them, they will break.

Cage Placement

Your gerbils should be part of your family. Place their cage in a location where you can watch and enjoy them. Make this a pleasant part of the room. The cage may be placed on a dresser or table with some attractive fabric beneath it. The floor is not the most ideal location, because the temperature there is often cooler than on a dresser or tabletop. A high shelf also is not ideal, because it will be too high for you to enjoy your pets. Over time, you will notice that your gerbils become less reactive to movements in the room. While at first they might retreat to their nest box whenever you walk by, eventually they will become tame and will continue with their activities.

Do not place your pets' home near a heating or air conditioning vent, a drafty window, or in direct sunlight. Gerbils can tolerate a house's normal variations in room temperature, light, and humidity, although ideal conditions consist of 60° to 70°F with a maximum relative humidity of 30 to 50 percent. They must be kept in a dry environment. Those who live in homes or cages with an environmental humidity greater than 50 percent will be stressed, and their fur will stand out and appear matted instead of smooth.

Gerbils who live in cold homes can become torpid and try to hibernate, something that you should prevent. Such cool temperatures are unlikely to occur in a home, but they could exist in a garage. Because of this, do not keep your gerbils in garages or basements. Not only are areas like this unhealthy due to automobile exhaust and dampness, but the temperature is more extreme and variable, both too cold and too hot. Most importantly,

The Stuff of Everyday Life

The Shavings Controversy

Shavings made from softwoods, which include pine and cedar, are still the most common type of bedding for small pets such as gerbils. These beddings have been popular because they are relatively inexpensive and are often fragrant smelling, particularly cedar shavings. The pleasant smell associated with these materials is due to the aromatic compounds found in the wood. However, cedar shavings have been implicated as both causing and aggravating respiratory problems in small animals. Few controlled, scientific studies have documented these problems. More common are reports that when a pet was removed from cedar shavings, his symptoms of poor health disappeared (such as sneezing). A few studies have shown that cedar shavings affect liver function in rats and mice, although the effect is so minute that it is only of concern to research scientists. Still, it has become common practice to recommend against cedar shavings for small pets.

Some hobbyists also argue that pine shavings are harmful. However, there is no scientific evidence supporting this assumption either. Research facilities across the country still house small animals on them. If there were any detrimental effects, scientists would be the first to switch beddings because they cannot afford to have their research animals harmed. Nonetheless, hobbyists report that pine shavings irritate their pets' respiratory system. If you wish to avoid the issue completely, you can use shavings made from hardwoods such as aspen and spruce. However, they tend to be more expensive than pine and are not available throughout the country. If you have no alternative to pine shavings, you can open the bag and let the aroma dissipate for a few days before using them in your gerbils' cage.

your gerbils are likely to be neglected.

Your pets' cage should be placed out of the direct view of the family cat or dog. Gerbils can become nervous and stressed if a large animal constantly sniffs and stares at them. They also might be sensitive to the ultrasonic sounds produced by computers and televisions. Therefore, do not place their home near electronics or appliances. In addition, because they are enthusiastic gnawers, do not leave any items such as clothing or papers on or near a wire frame cage—anything that can be pulled into it will be chewed and destroyed.

Provide your gerbils with fresh water from a gravity-fed water bottle.

Bedding

Your gerbils need bedding in their cage. Bedding is used to absorb moisture (from urine and water from the occasional leaking bottle), to reduce odors, and to provide a warm, dry place for your pets to sleep. This material also allows gerbils to engage in some natural behaviors, such as burrowing and building a sleeping nest. Pet stores carry a variety of small animal beddings that are suitable, including wood shavings such as pine and aspen, and more sophisticated beddings made from recycled paper or wood pulp that are designed to help control or eliminate odor. The latter types are more expensive, but they can make it more pleasurable to own gerbils because their home is less likely to smell unpleasant between cage cleanings. Bedding made from recycled paper contains no harmful inks, dyes, or significant levels of heavy metals. Whatever type you choose, provide a deep layer, about 4 inches (10.2 cm), so that your small pets can dig and burrow.

Bedding is an important component of your pets' environment, and it can affect their health. Ideally, it should be dust-free. Dusty materials can irritate a gerbil's respiratory system or aggravate an existing respiratory ailment. Because gerbils live directly on their bedding, they are more likely to stir up fine particles and be at risk for these potential problems. In general, paper pulp and recycled paper products tend to be lower in dust than wood shavings.

Odor Control

The ammonia vapors from urine that develop in your pets' cage can make owning gerbils less pleasant. The harsh smell is also uncomfortable for them. Ammonia is a severe irritant that is detrimental to their health. It affects the mucous membranes of their eyes and respiratory tract. With chronic respiratory conditions, your gerbils' health can worsen if exposure to ammonia vapors is constant, and it can make them more susceptible to opportunistic infections. Gerbils housed on dirty, moist bedding are most susceptible to these effects, as are gerbils housed in aquariums that are infrequently cleaned.

The development of innovative bedding products has been spurred by the quest to control or eliminate odor. Scientifically developed bedding made from a variety of materials, such as recycled paper, does not just mask odor; it is designed to reduce odor by

The Expert Knows

Activity Cycle

Unlike other small pets, such as hamsters, mice, and rats, gerbils are not nocturnal. They are crepuscular, which means that they are most active in the early morning and early evening. In other words, they are active when you are awake, ready at their cage door to come out and visit. Gerbils make many noises: gnawing, cracking seeds, drinking water, running on their exercise wheel, and playing with their other toys. While they are play-fighting with each other, you are likely to hear soft squeals and cheeps. When active at night, these busy nighttime noises might keep light sleepers awake. In between their active periods, your gerbils will snooze soundly, cuddled together in their nest box.

controlling the formation of ammonia. Such products promote a healthier environment for gerbils compared with traditional wood shavings and are highly recommended. If your pets are housed in an aquarium, if you are neglectful in cage cleaning, or if family members despise your pets because they smell, use innovative odor-controlling bedding.

Food Dishes

Place your pets' food in a dish. If you have a metal cage, you can attach it to the side to prevent it from tipping over

Homemade Toys

You can find suitable toys for your pets in your home. Give your gerbils the empty cardboard rolls from toilet paper or paper towels. You can partially bury these tubes under their bedding and create a system of tunnels for them to explore. Be creative and connect multiple rolls and make multiple entrances and exits. Cardboard (not Styrofoam) egg cartons also provide entertaining play for gerbils. They will chew on whatever you put in their cage, so be sure that the items are safe.

and to keep the contents from being spilled. If you use a free-standing dish, make sure that it is heavy enough so that your gerbils cannot tip it over. Pet stores sell a variety of colorful ceramic dishes that are too heavy for gerbils to move.

Using a dish can sometimes seem unnecessary because your gerbils will cart off favorite food items to store in their pantry. Nonetheless, placing their food in a dish instead of on the cage floor will prevent it from becoming accidentally contaminated with droppings and urine. Some hobbyists like to scatter food throughout the cage

to encourage more natural foraging behavior. It is best to use this method only if you keep the enclosure relatively clean at all times.

Water Bottles

Provide your gerbils with fresh water daily by using a gravity-fed water bottle sold at pet stores. A water bottle sold for hamsters is the best size to use for your gerbils. Choose a bottle with hatch marks (or make your own with an indelible marker) to help you monitor the amount of water your gerbils drink. They must always have clean water available. Ideally, you should empty and refill the water bottle every day, although most pet owners fill the bottle every other day.

The bottle's water tube should be at a comfortable height for your gerbils to easily reach up and drink from, but it should not be so low to the cage floor

Gerbils will enjoy playing with just about any safe toy that you put in their cage.

that bedding could contact the tube and cause the bottle to leak. To prevent leaks, the tip of the bottle should not touch the bedding or any cage furniture. A special holder, also available at pet stores, enables you to hang the water bottle in an aquarium. In case the bottle leaks, do not place it over your pets' food dish or near their nest box.

Do not use an open dish to provide water. Gerbils will fill the dish with their bedding, making the water unsanitary and unsuitable for drinking. Also, the increased moisture from a spilled dish of water can create an unhealthy, damp environment, especially in an aquarium-type cage.

Nest Boxes

Your gerbils need a nest box for sleeping and security. Keep in mind that many pet stores do not provide these hideaways for their small pets to make them easier for you to see. Because the animals are only in the store for a brief period of time, no harm is done. This "bedroom" gives your pets a safe hiding place to retreat away from loud noises and any disturbing activity outside their home.

You can buy a nesting box at any pet store. A variety of types are sold, including ones that are made to satisfy a small animal's natural instinct to chew, such as fruit-flavored cardboard tunnels, once the box becomes chewed up or smelly, you need to replace it.

Give your gerbils unscented tissue paper or paper towels to shred into nesting material. Shredding paper into a nest is a favorite activity for them. Pet stores also sell nesting material that you can use. Do not buy synthetic fiber bedding. The small fibers can wrap around a gerbil's feet, causing loss of the limb. Sometimes, gerbils eat the material and cannot pass it out of their system. Compressed nesting material made from cotton and sold for hamsters and other small animals is safe to use.

Toys

Toys give your gerbils something to do and will make them more enjoyable pets. With objects to play with, they are more active and interesting to watch, and they are content and happy. Without toys, gerbils become bored and listless. They will enjoy playing with almost anything you put in their cage. Their play involves scampering over the toys, darting in and out of tunnels, scent marking, and chewing. Expect your pets' playthings to be chewed and destroyed over time, so offer safe items and budget an "allowance" to buy new ones.

Clean your gerbils' cage before it starts to smell. Be sure to wash bowls, furnishings, and toys regularly.

huts made from natural plant fibers, and wooden blocks that a pet hollows out. Other kinds are less destructible and are made of ceramic or hard plastic. You also can make a nest box from an old cereal box or cardboard milk carton. However,

Pet stores sell a variety of toys that can be made into a playground for gerbils. You can give your pets toys designed for hamsters and other small rodents, such as wood chew sticks, tunnels, and ladders. If they are housed in an aquarium, you can increase the area available for them by adding ladders and platforms. Many wooden toys made for parakeets and parrots are safe to use with your gerbils. Wood chews keep them busy and active and provide a hard surface for them to gnaw, which helps to keep their teeth in good shape.

Tree branches from manzanita, willow, maple, ash, and apple trees are safe for chewing; just make sure that the trees were not treated with any kind of chemical. If safe branches are not readily available where you live, pet stores sell gerbil-safe limbs in their bird section. Wood toys absorb urine and other odors and need to be replaced when they become smelly and old.

Exercise Wheels

An exercise wheel is mandatory for gerbils. Most love exercise wheels and will enthusiastically run on them. They come in a variety of styles and sizes. Free-standing wheels made of either plastic or metal are sold for use in aquariums and wire cages. Because gerbils chew plastic, a metal wheel is your best choice. Occasionally, these pets have been known to get their feet or tails caught in wire frame exercise wheels. Therefore, buy one with a solid floor. It should measure at least 9 inches (22.8 cm) in diameter. If your pet has to arch his back while running in his wheel, he needs a larger one. Some exercise wheels develop an irritating squeak when a gerbil runs on them. A small drop of vegetable oil usually eliminates this problem.

Rotate Toys

Do not overcrowd the cage with toys. Not only does this leave little room for the gerbils, but they might become accidentally hurt if a toy falls on them. A gerbil might even lose part of his tail if it becomes trapped beneath a heavy toy. Alternating toys is a trick that dog and cat owners have used for years, and gerbil owners can use it as well. Let your gerbils play with a toy for a week, then take it away and replace

An empty cardboard paper towel roll can make a fun toy for your gerbils.

FAMILY-FRIENDLY TIP

A Parent's Role

Owning a pet is one of the pleasures of childhood. Besides being fun, it is even beneficial. A pet can teach children respect for other living creatures. They learn that a pet is not a toy and that he has needs separate from their own desires. For example, they should not handle the pet too much, and he must be allowed to sleep, even when they would rather take him out to play. Pets also allow children to assume responsibility and learn nurturing skills. They discover how to be compassionate, how to play gently, and what hurting means. Raising a pet from a young animal to adulthood can be a rewarding experience. Proud of their pets, kids enjoy the process of discovery that comes from caring for them.

However, these benefits are unlikely to occur without a parent's involvement. A child's age and maturity are important factors when deciding how much responsibility children can assume. Parents of younger children must know that the gerbils' welfare will be their responsibility, too. Many often tell their children, "Okay, you can get him, but don't expect me to help you care for him." However, depending on the child's age, this is an unrealistic expectation. While it is understandable that busy parents do not welcome additional responsibilities, the gerbils by themselves will not teach a child to be responsible. To a varying extent, a parent must participate in the care of a child's pet. Such assistance might include driving to the pet store to buy fresh food, supervising playtime to ensure the safety of the child and gerbils, or helping to clean a large cage that a small child has trouble managing.

Because children cannot be expected to care for their pets without supervision, it helps if a parent is enthusiastic about the pet. Unsupportive parents can make it more difficult for children to care for their gerbils properly.

it with a different one. The following week, temporarily take away this toy and replace it with the old one. By switching toys around, your gerbils will stay active and interested in exploring their environment.

Home Sweet Home

A clean home plays an important role in keeping your gerbils healthy. Gerbils are known among pet hobbyists as being able to go longer between cage cleanings than other small pets such as hamsters and mice. Some books recommend cage cleaning once every two weeks. If your pets are housed in a very large enclosure, such as a

Making Cage Cleaning Easier

Instead of feeling overwhelmed with the weekly task of cleaning and thus postponing it, try using a kitty litter scoop to quickly remove and replace some of the soiled bedding. Doing so allows the cage to remain sanitary a few extra days before you undertake a more meticulous cleaning. Another step to make cleaning easier is to buy larger quantities of bedding so that you always have some around for a quick change.

20-gallon (75.7 l) aquarium, then it is reasonable to consider cleaning once every two weeks. However, most gerbils are housed in much smaller enclosures. Even though the cage might not smell bad, you should clean it once a week.

During the course of a week, small, hard droppings will accumulate. Two gerbils can produce a lot of droppings in seven days, even if they are not obvious to you. They do not smell bad, but over time, urine can develop a pungent smell from ammonia. Ideally, you should clean your pets' cage before it becomes smelly. If the area around it smells offensive, it is past time to clean. And it is an unhealthy environment for your gerbils, especially because they are right on top of the smelly bedding all the time.

How to Clean the Cage

To clean your gerbils' cage, completely change the soiled bedding and replace it with fresh clean bedding. You can do a partial cage change between cleanings. Like other small pets, many gerbils will establish one or two toilet areas, which makes cage cleaning easier. If your pets use a corner for a bathroom area, replace the bedding in this area every few days or so. Doing so will help to reduce odor and keep the enclosure cleaner and more sanitary.

You can also try placing a litter pan in your gerbils' bathroom area. Pet stores sell small triangular animal litter pans that fit easily in corners. These litter pans usually are made for larger species of small pet such as rabbits and ferrets, but small models will fit inside a 10-gallon (37.9 l) home. Experiment to see if your gerbils will use a pan. Try placing it above the bedding in the cage, or see if they prefer it buried under the bedding. Use the same type inside the litter pan as in the rest of the cage. If your gerbils use the litter pan, it will be easier to clean the cage. When the pan is dirty, simply dump the soiled bedding and replace it with new. However, be aware that unlike cats, your gerbils will not consistently use it. The one drawback to a pan is that most are made of plastic and are likely to be eventually chewed and destroyed.

Each week, partially or completely (if it smells or is dirty) replace nesting material in the nest box as well. Also, you will need to wash or replace some of the toys and nest boxes when they become chewed and tattered, although you can do this less often. Sometimes these objects absorb urine odors and become smelly. Replacing them, rather than washing them, will greatly decrease any pungent smell.

While pet owners find a clean cage refreshing, gerbils are not as enthusiastic. They like something with their scent on it and will often become quite busy marking their home again so that it smells better to them. Partial cage cleanings, such as replacing most but not all of the bedding and nesting material and not washing all of the toys, will satisfy your gerbils' need for something familiar.

You must place your pets in a secure container, such as a plastic carrying cage, while you clean their home. Some owners place them in their nest box within the bathtub during cleaning. It provides a secure hiding place, and the slippery sides of the bathtub are usually too steep for gerbils to jump on or climb up.

Once a month, do a thorough cage cleaning. Wash it with hot, soapy water, and be sure to rinse and dry it completely. If necessary, disinfect the cage with a bleach solution. Immersing it for at least 30 seconds in a bleach solution consisting of 1 tablespoon (14.8 ml) of bleach for each gallon (liter) of cold water will kill any germs. Allow the cage to air dry afterward. Wash the water bottle, food dish, and any plastic toys. Wood toys can eventually splinter if washed in water; scraping them clean with a file is effective. Scrape or file off any grime that might have accumulated on the bars of a wire cage.

Chapter 3

Good Eating

With your gerbils' basic housing needs taken care of, it's time to discuss their diet. Proper nutrition is an important aspect of their daily needs, and it is essential to their good health.

Gerbils are herbivorous, which means that they eat the leaves, stems, and roots of plants, as well as seeds, fruits, berries, grains, and nuts. Omnivorous animals are those that eat both plant and animal foods. In the wild, gerbils snack on an occasional invertebrate, such as a spider or beetle, but many scientists still consider them herbivores. Similar nutritional requirements will need to be met in what they are fed in their new home habitat.

Basic Nutrition

Good nutrition is a key factor in promoting a long and healthy life for your pets. A balanced diet for gerbils includes the appropriate amounts of protein, carbohydrates, fats, vitamins, and minerals. All these nutrients interact in the building, maintenance, and functioning of a gerbil's body. It is also important to feed a diet that does not contain too much or too little of these nutrients. Feeding a healthy balanced diet is easy because a variety of appropriate commercial foods are sold at pet stores. Because gerbils have been used as laboratory animals for so many years, reliable information exists on their nutritional needs.

Proteins

Protein is needed for functions such as the growth and maintenance of muscle

Commercial foods provide a well-balanced diet for your gerbils.

It's important that food you feed your gerbils is fresh.

and the production of antibodies, hormones, and enzymes. The amount of protein that your pet needs is influenced by a number of physiological factors, such as age and reproductive status. Gerbils need less protein when they are adults than they do when they are growing or if they are pregnant or nursing a litter of babies. Experts do not agree on recommended protein levels. In general, the protein requirements for growing youngsters or breeding adults should be at least 16 percent and can be as high as 22 percent. Nonbreeding adults do well on as little as 12 percent protein, and gerbils older than two years can thrive on a diet of 10 to 12 percent protein.

Carbohydrates and Fats

Carbohydrates are used as a source of energy. Your gerbils will easily get enough carbohydrates with a diet based on seeds and grains, with most containing at least 50 percent carbohydrates.

Fats are a concentrated source of energy that provide twice as many calories per serving as proteins or carbohydrates. A good diet for gerbils should contain approximately 5 percent fat. Fats make up part of the structure of every cell and are necessary for the absorption of fat-soluble vitamins, including vitamins A, D, and E. Fats also help to prevent and alleviate skin problems. A deficiency of fat can show up as scaly skin or rough, thin hair. A good diet is typically no more than 10 percent fat.

Vitamins

Vitamins are necessary as catalysts for chemical reactions in the body. They are important in preventing diseases and in regulating functions such as growth and blood clotting. Vitamins are classified as water soluble or as fat soluble. A number of vitamins, such as vitamin B, are synthesized in gerbils by intestinal bacteria. These vitamins are made available to them by means of coprophagy: the eating of special droppings that contain the vitamins synthesized by the bacteria. Do not be concerned if you see your pets engaged in such behavior; leave them alone, because coprophagy is necessary for their good health.

Minerals

Minerals, which include calcium, phosphorous, sodium, and other chemical elements, are important in many body functions, such as the development of bones and teeth, muscle and nerve function, and proper water balance. A deficiency or excess can lead to serious medical problems. Trace elements, which include cobalt, copper, iodine, iron, manganese, selenium, and zinc, are necessary nutrients but only in very small amounts. Trace elements perform many functions, such as iron bringing oxygen to the body.

Food Freshness

Provide your gerbils with fresh food. Food that is old can become stale

Supplements

Feeding your gerbils a fresh, high-quality diet will usually ensure adequate intake of necessary vitamins and minerals. Supplementation with a vitamin and mineral supplement, unless directed by your veterinarian, is unnecessary.

and lose some of its nutritional value. Packaged foods should be fresh and sweet smelling, not rancid or dusty. Do not buy a large amount of food because it will take too long to use all of it.

Check to see whether an expiration date is on the package. Some manufacturers stamp a date on food bags and recommend that it be used within one year of this date. Typically, the freshest, best quality packaged food is found at busy pet and feed stores that constantly turn over their stock.

Proper storage of your pets' food is essential. It should be kept in a cool, dry environment. Exposure to sunlight, heat, and time degrade the vitamins in food. Keep it in an airtight container, such as a glass jar with a lid, or be sure to completely close a package that is self-sealing. This will keep the food fresh and prevent it from spoiling.

Packaged Food

You can feed your gerbils some of the rodent mixes sold at pet stores. These mixes contain seeds, grains, beans, nuts, alfalfa pellets, dried fruits and vegetables, and sometimes various types of kibble. Packaged foods typically contain all the nutrients your pets need to remain healthy. They are normally sold in packages marked for both gerbils and hamsters. The dietary requirements for both are similar, and foods sold for hamsters can usually be safely fed to gerbils. Do not choose a food that is mostly sunflower seeds or other nuts, because such a diet can lead to malnourishment and obesity.

Live Foods

Almost all gerbils enjoy chasing, catching, and eating live foods, which are a good source of protein and moisture. Crickets, mealworms, and waxworms are sold at pet stores for reptiles. It is fascinating to watch them pounce on a mealworm or chase after and catch a cricket to eat. A gerbil usually turns an insect in his hands so that he consumes the head first before eating the remainder of it. Your pets might appear to relish live food so much that you might be tempted to overindulge their appetites. But feed live foods as a treat, only one or two every few days. Not all gerbils will eat live foods; some become frightened and want nothing to do with the insect.

Different species of mealworm are sold in pet stores, some of which are giant sized. The larger type can put up quite a battle and will make your gerbils work for their food. Mealworms are beetle larvae. Any that escape can live in the cage, eventually pupate, and emerge as a beetle. Your gerbils can eat them at either of these two life stages.

You also can catch live moths for your pets from a porch light turned on at night in the summer. Many gerbils will eagerly expend quite a bit of energy chasing and catching the live moths that you put in their cage. If your pets live in a wire cage, pluck off one of the moth's wings to prevent it from flying out.

Gerbils enjoy picking through their food and eating their favorite items first. Because a food's nutritional analysis is based on consumption of the entire mix of ingredients, a selective eater may not be getting a nutritious, complete diet. Over time, this "selective feeding" can cause inadequate nutrition and obesity. While you should expect your gerbils to dislike some items in their food, consistently refusing to eat more than half of the ingredients is not healthy. Thwart selective feeding by not offering more food until your gerbils eat the less tasty items remaining in their food dish or pantry. You also can try offering a different brand of gerbil food that contains a more palatable blend of ingredients.

Reading Food Labels

Gerbil foods sold in pet stores are formulated to be nutritionally complete. The items that compose a food are stated in the ingredient's list and are presented in descending order by weight. The first three to five items on an ingredient list make up most of the food. Every bag of gerbil food should have a label that provides a guaranteed

Many gerbils enjoy eating and tunneling through hay.

health problems, such as obesity. For example, an overweight gerbil should be fed a food that is low in fat.

Laboratory Blocks

Consider feeding foods such as nutritionally complete pellets or laboratory blocks manufactured specifically for gerbils or other small rodents. These types of food contain a balance of all the nutrients that your pets need. They are convenient and easy to feed. Laboratory blocks have varying ratios of protein and fat, depending on the brand. The ingredients in these blocks are blended so that a gerbil cannot pick out one ingredient, and he will therefore consume adequate nutrients.

The texture of the blocks can influence how much your gerbils eat. The pellets and blocks are hard and help to keep the teeth trim. However, during cold, dry weather, they can become very hard, making them difficult for young gerbils to eat. During damp, humid weather, they may become soft. Stale pellets and blocks, which might be crumbly or soft, are not only less nutritious, but they are also less palatable to gerbils. Don't just feed laboratory blocks; your pets still need a gerbil mix so that they can engage in their natural behavior of hoarding food in their pantry.

Hay

Gerbils need fiber and many enjoy eating and tunneling through loose hay

analysis showing the percentage of each of the nutrients it comprises, such as protein, fat, fiber, and calcium, as well as fiber and moisture. The protein and fat contents are usually listed as minimums, while the amount of fiber and calcium are typically given as both minimums and maximums. The word "crude," which precedes each measure, refers to laboratory analysis rather than digestibility. Even commercial treats sold at pet stores provide basic nutritional information on protein, fat, fiber, and moisture content. Knowing the nutritional composition of a food can help you prevent and manage some rather than eating the alfalfa pellets found in most gerbil food mixes. Because the hay is dried, its moisture content is low and it can be free-fed. Besides essential fiber, hay gives your gerbil something to do. Place the hay on the floor of your pets' cage, or keep it in a hay rack that attaches to the side of a wire cage. You also can stuff some into a toilet paper tube. Making your gerbil work for his food helps to keep him active and healthy.

Most large pet stores sell a variety of hay in small, convenient packages. Look for hay products in the rabbit section of a pet store. There are two types of hay: Grass hay includes orchard grass, oat hay, timothy, and mixed grass, while legume hay includes alfalfa and clover. Gerbils usually prefer the tastier leaves and stems of alfalfa hay to grass hay. If loose hay is unavailable, try feeding cubed hay.

Gerbils also enjoy oat hay. They will gnaw on the stems and forage on the leaves and oat kernels. This type of hay is not usually available at pet stores, but it is sold by the bale at feed stores. A bale of hay is large—typically 4 feet (1.2 m) long by almost 2 feet (0.6 m) high and 2 feet (0.6 m) wide. Some feed stores may break one apart and let you buy several flakes; if not, you must buy the whole bale. The bale should be placed on a wooden pallet to allow air circulation and to prevent mold from growing on the bottom portion.

Coprophagy

Beneficial bacteria and protozoa, called microflora, live in the gerbil's digestive tract and help him digest food. These microorganisms produce various products or by-products of metabolism, including water-soluble vitamins and amino acids. These nutrients contribute substantially to a gerbil's nutrition. Some of the nutrients are directly absorbed in the gastrointestinal tract. However, many are not available to the gerbil unless he consumes special droppings that contain the nutrients synthesized by the bacteria, a practice called coprophagy.

Gerbils typically engage in this behavior at night or early in the morning when you are not likely to observe them. They eat the droppings directly

You can offer your gerbils small amounts of fresh fruits and vegetables a few times a week.

Your gerbils will greet with delight any treats that you give them, and tasty treats are a great way to win their confidence. It can be fun shopping for healthy treats in a pet store because there is such a great variety of delectable goodies just for small rodents. Commercial gerbil treats include honey-coated seed and nut sticks, dehydrated fruit and vegetable puffs, and nut cakes. Some come in attractive shapes and colors designed to appeal to people, not gerbils. Their packages often claim that the product is healthful and nutritious. However, many of these items, such as yogurt drops, are just like junk food for people and are high in fats, carbohydrates, and sugars. Only offer them on special occasions.

Moderation is the key when feed-ing treats. Your gerbils should not eat

so many that they have no appetite for their regular food. Some treats sold at pet stores are designed to help create a more interesting environment for your pets. Seed sticks, hay cubes, and millet sprays (in the bird section of pet stores) hung in the cage keep gerbils busy. To prevent overindulgence, hang the treats in the cage for five or ten minutes and then remove them. Offer them again the following day.

Other healthy treats to try include dry, unsweetened cereals such as toasted oats, crispy rice, and shredded wheat. Gerbils also enjoy pretzels, crackers, stale bread, hard, uncooked noodles, uncooked rice, and uncooked hot cereals (for example, cracked four-grain cereal). Many love dog biscuits, but be cautious about offering any of your dog's regular kibble because some brands are high in fat. These treats and the hard foods in your gerbils' regular diet will help to keep their teeth trim.

If your pets are housed in a wire cage, do not feed them treats through the cage bars. Otherwise, anything (including a finger) that is poked through might get nipped. Always open the cage door to offer a treat. In addition, wash your hands before handling your gerbils because any food smells on your hands can cause your pets to nip.

from the anus, so normally you will never see them. Nonetheless, do not be concerned if you see your pets engaged in such behavior. Leave them alone, because coprophagy is necessary for their good health. Although this seems unpleasant, digesting the food a second time allows your gerbils to obtain the most nutrition from their food. Cows also digest their food a second time, but they chew cud that comes up from their stomach.

Vegetables and Fruits

In addition to your gerbils' regular diet of grains, seeds, hay, and laboratory blocks, offer them small amounts of fresh fruits and vegetables a few times a week. Gerbils enjoy fruits and vegetables, and these foods provide important variety and nutrients in their diet.

Before offering these items, be sure to wash and dry them. You can use a small piece of tasty vegetable or fruit to bond with your pets during playtime and training.

Fruit and vegetable treats should be small enough that your gerbils are able to comfortably hold them in their paws. Offer no more than ¼ teaspoon. By adhering to this conservative estimate, they are less likely to experience any problems such as diarrhea. Ideally, your gerbils should immediately eat fresh food items. If not eaten right away, they could spoil. Check your pets' pantry and nest about 30 minutes after giving them these treats and remove any uneaten items. Moist food left in the cage can become putrid. Bacteria and mold can grow on it, which could make your gerbils sick. Hard vegetables and fruits such as carrots and apples are less likely to spoil than soft, moist items like cucumbers and berries.

Offer previously untried food in very small pieces to make sure that your gerbils like it and to ensure that it will not cause digestive upset. Feeding a large amount could lead to digestive upset and cause diarrhea. Feed only one type of vegetable or fruit at a time, and wait several days before offering another kind. This way you will know if a particular item causes problems. If a vegetable or fruit does cause diarrhea, do not feed it again. If you have not offered fruits or vegetables in a while, always err

Unhealthy Foods

While it's fun to offer your gerbils new types of food and see if they enjoy them, not all foods are good for them. What shouldn't you feed your gerbils? Do not feed them dry cat food, which is too high in protein. Seed and nut mixes sold for parrots and cockatiels should also be avoided due to the high fat content of the nuts. Also, do not feed your pets junk food made for people. Although gerbils will happily eat potato chips and eagerly look for more, potato chips, cookies, candy, chocolate, and other snack foods are not healthy for your pets.

on the safe side by offering very tiny amounts.

Gerbils enjoy a variety of vegetables, including carrots, broccoli, peas, spinach, squash, peppers, corn, tomatoes, beets, celery, red peppers, avocados, and fruits such as apples, bananas, apricots, peaches, plums, and berries. Also offer small amounts of dried fruits such as banana chips and raisins, as well as dehydrated vegetables such as carrots and peas. Remove the seeds of apples, which are poisonous, before feeding your pets. You also should remove

any large seed pits before feeding the fruit to your pet. Although the pits can help your gerbil keep his teeth trim, the "nut" inside the hard shell can sometimes be poisonous, as is the case with apricot pits.

Some gerbils also like green wheat shoots (sold as cat greens at pet stores). In addition, they enjoy fresh dandelion greens, including the yellow flowers. If you opt to feed your pets dandelions, obtain them from a location free of pesticides and herbicides. Wash and dry them as you would lettuce, and offer only a small piece each day. Leafy greens should be no more than about 1 inch by 1 inch (2.5 by 2.5 cm) in size.

Nutty for Nuts

Gerbils love nuts, especially the sunflower seeds in food mixes. Scientists use their extreme fondness for nuts when they need to use food

The amount a gerbil eats will depend on the kind of food you feed him.

Feeding Schedule

Feed your gerbils the same amount of food at the same time each day. Because gerbils are active during both the day and night, you can select a feeding time that best suits your schedule. Many pet owners prefer to feed their gerbils when they come home from school or work. Your gerbils will begin to anticipate feeding time and become more active while waiting for their food. Each day, you must discard the old food in their dish and replace it with fresh food. The obvious satisfaction and delight that gerbils take when eagerly sorting through a fresh dish of food makes feeding a rewarding time to observe your pets. Watching them eat, even for a few minutes, will help you determine that they are active and well.

to motivate them in various studies. Dozens of types are available, and your pets will enjoy them all, including pine nuts, walnuts, peanuts, cashews, and Brazil nuts. Don't feed salted nuts, though; raw ones are best. You also can offer nuts inside their shell. In some cases, you might need to partially crack the shell so that your gerbils can smell the nut meat. Besides the ones in their regular food, only feed nuts as special treats and only in small, gerbil-sized amounts. Nuts are fatty, and too many will cause these tiny animals to become overweight. If allowed to only

eat nuts, gerbils will become susceptible to a variety of other health problems, including bone fractures, trouble with bone development, growth problems, and a shorter life span.

Moist Foods That You Shouldn't Feed

There are some vegetables that you should not feed your pet because they can cause gastrointestinal upset. Even if your gerbil seems to eat these vegetables without noticeable problems, it is still best not to include them because they can cause digestive problems. Fresh foods that you should avoid feeding include iceberg lettuce, raw kidney beans, onions, raw potatoes, and rhubarb. Also, be aware that many houseplants are poisonous to gerbils. Never give your pet any part of a houseplant to snack on.

How Much to Feed

How much your gerbils need to eat will change throughout their lives, and the amount will vary according to their age, gender, and activity level. Young growing gerbils need to eat more food per gram of body weight than adults. Also, because males are larger than females, they need to eat more food.

55

Kids Can Help With Feeding

Parents should not give their children tasks that are too difficult. Preschool-age children (three to five years) can help with simple tasks such as pouring premeasured food into the gerbils' dish. Elementary-age children (six to nine years) can assume more responsibility. For example, they can feed and water the gerbils and remind their parents when fresh supplies are needed. Usually, children ten years of age and older can assume almost full responsibility for their pets' daily needs, although their parents should still oversee care to make sure that they do not neglect their pets.

However, pregnant and nursing females need to eat more food than males. Gerbils who run around and play with regularly rotated toys will require more nourishment than those who just sit in their cage with little to do. Unless you weigh the amount of food that you feed, you are unlikely to notice these differences because they are very small.

The amount that your gerbils eat also will vary depending on the type of food that you feed. Typically, they eat less of the laboratory blocks than they do of the rodent mixes. Most stop eating when they have consumed enough calories. Your gerbils should feel solid and sleek without any extra padding on their sides from fat. Any marked decrease in appetite could signal illness.

Because gerbils like to nibble on food throughout the day and night, ensure that they always have food in their dish or in their pantry. If the bowls are empty, increase the amount of food you feed. Conversely, if your gerbils' food pantry becomes too large, you are feeding too much. Every few days, check to ensure that the food is not damp or moldy, and discard stored food at each weekly cleaning.

Hoarding Fresh Food in the Pantry

Pay attention when feeding your gerbils fresh food, because some will hide a piece of vegetable or fruit in their nest. If they do not eat the food right away, it could spoil. You must remove any uneaten fresh foods every day before offering your pets additional items. If fresh foods are constantly left over, you are probably feeding your gerbils too much and should reduce the amount you feed. Ideally, your gerbils should consume fresh foods right away.

Water

Always provide your gerbils with fresh, clean water. The amount of water that gerbils drink each day depends on the moisture in their food. If you provide them with small amounts of fresh fruits, vegetables, and live insect foods, they will drink less water than if they ate only dry foods. Wild gerbils are able to extract water from the foods they eat as well as by licking dew from plants and rocks in the early morning. Gerbils further conserve water by concentrating their urine, an adaptation to their original desert home.

Even though wild gerbils do not drink much, domesticated ones must always have water available. Compared to other small pets, such as mice, gerbils drink comparatively little water. An adult female will drink between 2.8 to 5.7 milliliters of water a day compared to the 3.3 to 5.7 milliliters that a male will drink each day. Females drink less because they are smaller than males; they weigh between 55 and 85 grams compared to males, who weigh between 65 and 100 grams. In comparison, a 40-gram mouse will drink 6 milliliters of water a day. So even though gerbils weigh more than mice, they still drink less water each day. As gerbils get older, they drink more water. Because they drink such a small amount each day, you might not notice this increase.

Select a water bottle that is large enough so that your gerbils do not run out of water. The standard hamster bottle provides sufficient water to last two gerbils for most of the week. Many are sold with milliliter or ounce markings on them. (There are approximately 29.5 milliliters in 1 ounce.) Such markings are useful to track water consumption. If the amount of water in the bottle does not seem to decrease over a day or so, check to see whether the metal spout is clogged with bedding.

Ideally, change the water every few days. However, most pet owners do not find this practical or convenient. At the very least, completely change the water once a week. It might be necessary to change it more often if you have more than two gerbils in a cage. Because gerbils drink such little water, some owners neglect this task because they assume that the water is still fresh, but it can become stale and contaminated with bacteria and other harmful pathogens.

Give the water bottle a good cleaning at least once a week. Even if it looks clean, it is probably slimy on the inside. Use a slender bristle brush to clean the slimy residue coating the bottle. Check to see that the stopper is not clogged. Some gerbils nibble the metal water spout. Also, check to be sure that there are no jagged ends that could cut your pets. If there are, you will need to replace the water bottle and drinking tube.

Always provide your gerbils with fresh, clean water.

Looking Good

If you are looking for pets who require little in the way of grooming, gerbils are a good choice. These tiny rodents are naturally clean and need very little, if any, assistance from you to stay that way. Nevertheless, whether a minor or major chore, grooming is part of your responsibility as a pet owner, and it will keep your gerbils looking good and feeling good. The hands-on routine will also give you an opportunity to bond with them, as well as allow you to detect any changes in their appearance or body that may signal a health problem.

Brushing

Sometimes the hair around a gerbil's belly gland may appear wet or greasy, but this is nothing to be concerned about. All furry animals shed hair, your gerbils included. Some fur colors, such as nutmeg, start out as one color and then molt into another color. This color change lets you know that your pet is shedding. However, a gerbil's hair is so short and fine that you are unlikely ever to notice any shed hair in or near your pet's cage. If you wish, you can gently brush your pets using a small, soft kitten brush or a toothbrush. Although unnecessary, brushing can be an enjoyable way to bond with your gerbil. Some like the attention, while others do not. If your gerbils remain still while you gently brush them, assume they like it, but if they always struggle and run away, it should be obvious that they do not like being brushed.

Gerbils are naturally clean; they spend much of their waking time grooming themselves. A gerbil uses his front paws to wash his face, delicately cleans each ear with his hind toes, nibbles clean his toes, washes his front and backside, and even grooms his long furry tail. Gerbils also groom each other, especially in hard-to-reach places like the neck and back. A gerbil who cannot keep himself clean is probably sick and should be examined by a veterinarian.

Dust Baths

What do you wash with if no water is available? The answer is sand, which

Grooming Supplies

These are the supplies you'll need to keep your gerbils looking their best:

- chinchilla dust
- cotton swabs
- scissors
- small animal nail clippers
- soft bristle brush
- styptic powder
- towel

is readily available in a gerbil's natural habitat. Like many wild animals, wild gerbils take dust baths to keep themselves clean and to control external parasites. Adults take dust baths more often than juveniles. Because gerbils leave their scent where they roll in dust, taking dust baths might be a means of communicating with other gerbils.

Pet gerbils also like dust baths, and they can be quite entertaining to watch. Use chinchilla dust (usually volcanic ash) or bird gravel for this

Grooming for Good Health

A regular grooming routine can help you maintain your pets' health as well as his appearance. When you groom your gerbils, take time to inspect their bodies and overall condition:

- Monitor their weight: Do they feel too thin, too fat, or just right?

- Examine the coat and body: Are there any bald spots or any unusual lumps or bumps since you last groomed them?

- Check their teeth: Are they in good condition or are they overgrown?

- Check their eyes, ears, and nose: Do they have discharge from any or all of them?

Knowing what's normal for your pets and noticing changes in their appearance and routine are the first steps in maintaining good health. If you find something unusual, contact your veterinarian. It's much easier to treat minor problems before they become serious health issues.

Your gerbils will never need a bath with water and shampoo.

purpose. Use a container that's deep enough to hold about ½ inch (1.27 cm) of dust and large enough so that they can somersault and flip around in the dust. A glass or hard plastic container with sides about 2 inches (5.1 cm) high works well. Place the dust bowl in the cage for a short time every few days. Replace the dust after two or three baths.

Bathing

Your gerbils will never need a bath with water and shampoo. Washing them can cause them to get sick, even if you use warm water and dry them with a towel. Using a hair dryer is even

worse because you can accidentally burn your pets, not to mention increase their stress level astronomically—so don't do it! If one of your gerbils has gotten into something sticky, he usually can clean his coat by himself. If necessary, help his grooming by carefully trimming away any sticky hair. To prevent accidentally cutting his skin, do not use scissors larger than the small type made for cutting people's nails. You also can spot-clean his sticky fur with the corner of a warm, damp washcloth. Immediately use a paper towel or a dry cloth to absorb the moisture.

No matter how much a gerbil grooms himself, if he has been living on dirty bedding, he will not be able to keep himself smelling clean. Instead of a bath, clean the cage, provide fresh, sweet-smelling bedding, and allow your gerbils to groom themselves. Clean cages are one of the most important ways that you can help your gerbils stay clean and well groomed.

Nail Care

Just like your nails, a gerbil's nails grow continuously. It's not necessary to trim your pets' nails to keep them healthy and happy, unlike other small pets such as rabbits and guinea pigs, whose nails must be routinely trimmed. Most gerbils chew and clip their own nails to keep them short. While their nails can be sharp, you should rarely notice them if you properly handle your pets.

A gerbil's nails sometimes become caught in the wire floor of a cage or on a carpet. During his struggles, the nail can rip or tear by the root. The damaged nail bed often turns black, but it usually heals on its own. Sometimes the nail will regrow, while in other cases, the nail will never regrow. This is not a cause for concern unless you notice redness or swelling of the toe, which could indicate an infection.

If you think that your gerbils need their nails cut, have a veterinarian perform the procedure and show you how to do so. Cutting a gerbil's nails often can be difficult, and if done improperly, painful and traumatic. Because gerbils are so small and wiggly, it is very easy to slip and accidentally cut the toe. Gerbils must be restrained during nail cutting, and you don't want your pets to associate you with this unpleasant experience.

Nonetheless, if you think it is necessary to cut your pets' nails, use clippers designed for birds or cats. Make sure that the clippers are sharp because it will make the task much easier. Keep cotton swabs and some type of styptic powder nearby to stop any bleeding. The best time to trim your gerbils' nails is when they are sluggish and sleepy, not when they are wide awake. Two people are necessary—one person to hold the gerbil and the other to clip the nails. The individual who holds

Have your vet show you how to cut your gerbils' nails.

63

be cut below the quick. If it is trimmed too short, painful bleeding will occur and your gerbil will bite. One quick, small cut is adequate, just enough to remove the sharp, pointed tip. If your gerbil's nail begins to bleed, blot it with the cotton swab and then treat it with styptic powder.

Ear Care

Gerbils can keep their ears clean without any help from you. The only time you need to examine their ears is if you notice them scratching excessively at them or if they appear red and inflamed. Gerbils rarely get ear mites. However, if left untreated, mite infestations can cause serious problems. Take a gerbil to a veterinarian if you notice excessive scratching, heavy wax buildup, discharge, redness, swelling, or odor. Your veterinarian must diagnose

Grooming Guidelines

Children can help groom gerbils by gently brushing them under adult supervision. After demonstrating that they can handle the animals carefully without harming them, they can be allowed to groom them regularly. Children can also look at gerbils' eyes or ears to see if they need cleaning and let an adult know if this type of attention is needed. Responsibilities can be added as the child matures.

Gerbils

the gerbil should be the person with whom the gerbil is most familiar. Pet the gerbil, talk softly to him, and keep your hands away from his mouth in case he is accidentally hurt and bites.

Before attempting to cut your gerbil's nails, know where the quick ends, which is the living portion of the nail that contains nerves and blood vessels. The quick is sometimes hard to detect in gerbils with dark-colored nails, but if you look underneath the nail, you usually can see where it ends. The nail should

Changes in your gerbils' appearance or body may signal a health problem.

ear mites using a microscope because they are not visible to the naked eye. Veterinarian-prescribed medication will eliminate the condition but must be continued for several weeks to kill all stages of the mites' life cycle. Do not automatically assume that any discharge is from ear mites and treat your pet with an ear mite medication sold at pet stores. The most effective treatment and advice for remedying the problem is only available from a veterinarian. Accurate diagnosis of the condition will speed your gerbil's recovery and save him from discomfort and pain.

Regular grooming will keep your gerbils looking and feeling their best.

Chapter 5

Feeling Good

When purchased from a good source and provided
with proper loving care, gerbils are hardy little
animals who infrequently get sick. Most pet gerbils
live a healthy life without ever requiring a visit
to the veterinarian. They do not need an annual
"wellness exam" and they do not require any
vaccinations. In fact, gerbils do not appear to be
prone to as many potential ailments as other
small pets.

Although this section describes common gerbil ailments, it is no substitute for sound veterinary care. If you suspect that your pet is sick, take him to a veterinarian right away.

Finding a Veterinarian

For a gerbil to receive the proper treatment, a correct diagnosis of his condition is necessary. A veterinarian who routinely treats rodents and has a special interest in their care is best qualified and will most likely have the necessary gerbil-sized equipment. Such individuals are more likely to be aware of advances and changes in treatment protocol. To locate a veterinarian who is knowledgeable about rodents, call different veterinarians' offices and ask if they will treat gerbils. You also can inquire at pet stores, critter clubs, and humane societies.

Even if you don't expect your gerbils to ever need a veterinarian's care, accidents happen that can require immediate medical attention for your injured pet. This is why it's important to take five minutes and find a veterinarian who treats rodents before you need one. Not all vets will treat these small pets, and you do not want to waste time in an emergency calling around to find a gerbil doctor.

Cost

Even when you recognize that one of your gerbils is "under the weather," you might hesitate to take him to a veterinarian

Find a veterinarian who is familiar with treating small animals.

Taking proper care of a sick gerbil can help his recovery. Keep an ill pet in a warm, quiet area, and monitor his water and food intake. A heating pad made for pets (sold in the reptile section of pet stores) placed outside and under one half of the cage can provide additional warmth. Do not place the heating pad inside the cage! Regularly monitor the cage temperature to be sure that it does not exceed 86°F (29.4°C).

Make sure that a sick gerbil has easy access to food and water. If he has trouble moving, lower the water bottle so that he can easily reach the sipper, and place his food on the bedding rather than in his dish.

Carefully administer any medications that your veterinarian prescribes. Inform her if your gerbil is constipated or has diarrhea that seems related to the treatment. Do not attempt to treat him

yourself with human medications or antibiotics bought at a pet store. Many of these medications are poisonous to gerbils and will kill your pet.

After any kind of surgery, keep your gerbil's cage clean to prevent any secondary bacterial infections at the surgery site. Check the incision site each day for swelling or discharge. Also, monitor whether your gerbil is chewing the stitches. Be sure to consult your veterinarian if your pet has not eaten or defecated within 24 hours of returning home.

During treatment, it might be necessary to separate your gerbils from one another if your sick pet needs quiet rest. The veterinarian will let you know whether this is required. However, this can be stressful to your gerbils, and it also can be difficult to put them back together again after the sick gerbil is well. Removal for a contagious disease should not be necessary because both gerbils must be treated, even if one does not look sick. If separation is recommended—for example, if one gerbil is chewing on the other's stitches—try dividing the cage into two halves so that the gerbils are still next to

If your gerbil shows a change in behavior, such as no interest in food, he may be ill.

due to the potential expense. A visit to a veterinarian can be costly, and it can be difficult to spend large sums of money on a gerbil who cost very little to begin with. Some owners will spend whatever it takes to treat their well-loved pets, but others cannot afford to do so. Discuss potential costs with your veterinarian beforehand so that you will have a better idea of the expense of your gerbil's care. Although it might be difficult to put a price on your pet, in some cases it might be necessary to decide how much you can afford to spend.

Be cautious about seeking advice from friends, pet store employees, or the Internet before taking your sick gerbil to a veterinarian. Although they may be helpful and can assist you in making an educated guess, the expertise, diagnostic skills, and medication needed to treat your pet are only available from a veterinarian.

The Vet Visit

If you do need to take one of your gerbils to the veterinarian, be prepared to describe his housing and what you feed him. If the cage is small enough and you can temporarily rehouse your other pets, use it to transport him to the veterinarian. This is often less stressful because your gerbil remains in his familiar home. If the cage is too large, use a plastic small animal habitat sold at pet stores. Place some of your pet's soiled bedding in the carrying cage as well as a cardboard tube or nest box in which your gerbil can hide. Partially covering his regular cage or carrying cage with a towel will help him feel more secure.

Because dogs and cats will likely be in the veterinary clinic's waiting room, it is best to wait to bring your pet into the clinic until the veterinarian is ready to see you. After checking in, remaining with your pet in a temperature-controlled car can reduce the stress he will feel when he senses these potential predators.

A Sick Pet

You will learn how your pets behave when they are frightened or excited, how they react to new situations, and what it means when they assume different postures. Knowing a gerbil's normal behavior will help you recognize when one of your pets might be sick. For example, gerbils enjoy regular feeding and playing times. A sudden lack of interest in these things could mean that your pet is ill and you should consult a veterinarian.

General Signs of Illness

Experienced pet owners and breeders are adept at recognizing when a pet is sick. As you gain experience caring for your pets, especially if you develop a long-term interest, you also will become more proficient at it. Sick gerbils generally present a similar range of symptoms. They are fastidious and keep themselves clean. Any discharge from the eyes or nose that a gerbil cannot keep washed away should be considered an obvious sign of illness. In some cases, the discharge is often visible on the paws as a result of his grooming efforts.

Sudden changes in behavior, such as lethargy and reduced appetite, also can indicate illness. Signs of disease that are more difficult to detect include rough, unkempt hair, hunched posture, and weight loss. Pay particular attention if your gerbil is sensitive when touched on a certain part of his body, because this could indicate an injury from being dropped or squeezed. A gerbil who huddles by himself, away from his buddy, is probably sick. Any of these symptoms suggest that something might be wrong, and a visit to the veterinarian is prudent.

Note to Parents

Gerbils often seem to tolerate a dirty environment. This trait is beneficial because they are primarily children's pets and often suffer from occasional neglect. However, although gerbils are hardy creatures, their tolerance can eventually diminish and they will become sick if kept in an unsanitary environment.

Act Fast

Most gerbils who are sick, especially with diarrhea, need to be immediately treated by a veterinarian. This is especially important because owners often do not notice symptoms until the animal is very ill. By the time you realize that your gerbil is ill, he has usually been sick for quite some time. In many cases, treatment is difficult because the condition is so advanced at the time of detection. Although some diseases progress rapidly and an affected pet can die within 24 hours, early recognition of a sick animal may make the difference between life and death. Furthermore, keep in mind that the sicker a gerbil is, the more likely he is to be traumatized from the procedures at a veterinarian's office.

Emergency Symptoms

If your gerbil is displaying signs of illness or just doesn't seem to be acting like his normal frisky self, take him to the veterinarian for a checkup. The vet will be able to diagnose any medical problem.

The following symptoms indicate the need for immediate emergency care. Don't wait to see what happens, or it could be too late:

- appears to be in pain when handled
- bleeding

Minimizing stress can help to keep your gerbil healthy.

Groups of gerbils housed together can injure each other in a fight.

- cold, listless to the touch
- constipation
- diarrhea
- paralysis
- protruding, broken bone
- rapid or labored breathing
- refusing to eat or drink
- sitting hunched, reluctant to move
- weepy, crusty eyes
- weight loss

Stress

Stress is a catchall word for a variety of conditions that disturb or interfere with a pet's normal physiological equilibrium. Because stress often leads to illness, it is frequently mentioned as a detrimental, contributing factor to various diseases. Besides becoming sick, a gerbil can exhibit signs of stress in other ways, such as seizures, lack of appetite, hair loss, and loose droppings. It is useful for pet owners to be aware of what constitutes stress for their gerbils.

A gerbil can experience stress from pain and fear, when moving to a new cage, from a change in diet, exposure to temperature fluctuations, and/or an environmental humidity that is too high. The trip from a pet store or breeder to a new home can be frightening and stressful as well. Once in their new home, some gerbils settle down right away, while others take longer to adjust. Until they are

Antibiotics

Infectious diseases that are caused by bacteria are treated with antibiotics. Gerbils are sensitive to the effects of antibiotics. Some can be harmful because they completely destroy or alter the useful bacteria that normally live in a gerbil's digestive system (sometimes referred to as good bacteria or gut flora). Both conditions can lead to death.

You don't need to worry about which antibiotics are safe for your gerbil. Your veterinarian will know what types can be safely used, as well as the recommended dosages for every condition. Some antibiotics must be placed in your pet's water. If so, you must empty and wash the water bottle and stopper each day during the treatment before adding the new medication. Carefully monitor your pet while he is being treated with an antibiotic, and immediately report any decline in health to your veterinarian. Some owners provide a small amount of live culture yogurt following treatment with an antibiotic to help reestablish good bacteria. Whether doing so helps is unknown, but it does not seem to cause any harm.

tame, some gerbils become stressed when held. Other stressful situations include loud noises, changes in diet, overcrowding, and harassment by dogs, cats, ferrets, or other pets.

Groups of gerbils housed together can fight and injure each other. Fighting and bullying is particularly stressful for the animal that is always picked on because he is at the bottom of the pecking order. Stress also can be a major factor in the development of what might otherwise remain a dormant disease. Therefore, it is wise to minimize the stress in your gerbils' lives.

Gerbil Ailments

The ailments that might affect gerbils can be classified into four categories: trauma-induced injuries, infectious diseases, noninfectious diseases, and improper husbandry. The reasons that a gerbil becomes sick are often a combination of factors from more than one category. For example, a poorly ventilated cage can create a noxious-smelling environment with high levels of ammonia that causes an outbreak of a latent respiratory disease. Numerous factors affect how sick the gerbil will get. These factors include the virulence of the pathogen, age, dietary deficiencies, and whether the gerbil is already sick with another illness.

Trauma-Induced Injuries

A traumatic injury occurs when a gerbil is dropped, sat on, squashed behind a door or a piece of furniture, falls from a height, or is squeezed while being held. When a gerbil has a traumatic injury, it is usually obvious. Trauma can be easier to treat than infectious diseases because it is easier to detect. The animal is often in acute and immediate pain and distress. If a gerbil is injured, especially if he appears in pain, bring him to a veterinarian right away. She can determine whether the injury can be treated or whether it is kinder to put the gerbil out of his misery through euthanasia.

Abscesses

An abscess is usually due to the secondary bacterial infection of a bite wound inflicted during a fight, or it could be caused by the infection of a cut. Some experienced gerbil breeders are able to treat abscesses by using pressure to drain them. However, this can be gruesome, and a veterinarian is the preferred route to tend to an abscess.

Using a needle, the veterinarian will biopsy (or sample) the abscess, then drain and clean the site. Usually a topical antibiotic is applied to the area. The bacteria that cause an abscess are often opportunistic and can infect other organs besides the skin, so it is important that an affected gerbil be properly treated. A veterinarian might deem it necessary to culture, or grow, a sample of the fluid to identify the type of bacteria present. An antibiotic selected on the basis of culture and sensitivity test results is likely to be highly effective.

Broken Bones

Broken bones are a potential hazard because gerbils are wiggly and can accidentally jump from your hands if something frightens them. They also do not judge distances from heights very well and can easily tumble off a table or bed. Properly holding and playing with your pets can prevent such injuries from occurring. Trauma injuries to legs and toes usually heal naturally and get better without special care. However, if your pet appears to be in pain or a broken bone is protruding, he must be taken to a veterinarian immediately. In some cases, an experienced veterinarian can splint the broken bone.

Parasites

Parasites are organisms that survive by living and feeding on other organisms. In the wild, gerbils are hosts to numerous species of fleas. However, when obtained from a reputable source and kept in a clean environment, gerbils do not typically have parasites. However, if your dog or cat has fleas, then it is possible for your gerbils to get fleas.

Scratching is the most obvious symptom. You also might see the fleas or observe their dark droppings. Depending on the brand, a flea treatment approved for use on kittens can be safe to use on your gerbils. However, always check with your veterinarian as to whether the product should be used. Besides treating your gerbils, you also must treat the cage and surroundings, as well as other family pets.

Occasionally, gerbils can be infested with mites. In an aquarium, you might notice the mites walking on the glass walls. The route of transmission could be contaminated food or bedding. Your vet will prescribe an effective treatment and review how to prevent another infestation from occurring. As with other external parasites, usually both the gerbils and their cage must be treated.

Injuries From Fights

Injuries from fighting sometimes occur. Occasionally, an established pair of gerbils becomes aggressive and fights with each other. Scabs around the tail, head, throat, and belly usually mean that a fight has occurred. The loser is the one with the most wounds. If you are present when the gerbils are locked in combat, use a towel or glove to separate them. If one of them is badly injured or the fighting continues over several days, you will probably need to keep them in separate cages.

Because infection from bacteria is always possible when a gerbil is bitten in a fight, clean any bloody injuries with warm water and an antiseptic. Wounds from bites usually form scabs and heal without further care. However, an abscess can develop at the site of a bite due to bacterial infection. Watch the wound, and if you detect any prolonged swelling or sign of redness, take your gerbil to the veterinarian.

Tail Loss

Don't pick up your gerbil by his tail. Like lizards, gerbils can lose a portion of their tail. If you grab or hold your pet by his tail, you are likely to be left holding a piece of skin and fur. The skinless portion of the tail will die and fall off. Usually the stump will heal on its own and not become infected. On rare occasions, a vet might need to amputate a portion of the tail if it does not heal properly. Your pet gerbil can live a normal life with a short tail.

Infectious Diseases

Infectious diseases can spread from one animal to another and are caused by bacteria, viruses, and protozoa. Sometimes, the diseases caused by these agents are subclinical, meaning that signs of infection are difficult to detect. Individual animals also differ in their resistance to infectious organisms. Some exposed animals never display any symptoms. However, stress or other bacterial or viral infections can cause an animal to suddenly show symptoms. A single pet is less at risk for infectious diseases compared to a pet that is housed in close proximity to large numbers of other animals of the same species. Infectious diseases are often preventable through good husbandry.

Respiratory Ailments

Respiratory ailments are most common in young and newly weaned gerbils, not adult gerbils. Affected animals tend to be lethargic. If you hold your gerbil up to your ear and can hear a clicking noise made by mucus in his nasal passages as he breathes, he needs prompt veterinary care and treatment with antibiotics. The vet will let you know if the sick gerbil's buddy also should be treated.

Sore Nose

One of the most common health problems in gerbils is nose dermatitis or sore nose. Hair loss, bloody secretions, and moist infected skin on the muzzle and nose of gerbils are symptoms of this condition. A loss of hair from the snout can start from self-inflicted trauma—for example, if a gerbil constantly rubs his nose on

77

Signs of Dental Problems

- difficulty eating
- excessive salivation (slobbers)
- inability to close jaw
- nasal or eye discharge
- poor coat condition
- reduced food intake
- weight loss

the bars of a wire cage. Some experts believe that irritation from coarse bedding or an allergy to the bedding causes the initial symptoms. Sometimes, changing the bedding, for example, from corn cob to aspen, will help to resolve the condition.

Other forms of this disease are caused by an increase in secretions from the Harderian gland and are complicated by a bacterial infection. Many believe that excessive Harderian gland secretions are irritating to a gerbil's skin, which then becomes infected with the

bacteria. Excessive Harderian gland secretion is associated with stress, and this condition tends to affect young gerbils.

Whatever the initial cause, if bacteria are involved, nose dermatitis will not get better by itself. Left untreated, the hair loss and red scabs will spread from the head to other parts of the body such as the legs and belly. The affected area will be itchy, and frequent scratching can cause bleeding. Your veterinarian is best qualified to diagnose and treat skin conditions and can prescribe any necessary antibiotics. Providing your gerbil with fresh sand for a daily dust bath also can aid his recovery.

78

Gerbils

Hobbyists are trying to reduce the incidence of inherited conditions like seizures.

Tyzzer's Disease

This is a highly contagious disease that is caused by bacteria (*Clostridium piliforme*). Tyzzer's disease must be caught and treated early because it is usually fatal. Symptoms include a scruffy coat, lack of activity, diarrhea, loss of appetite, hunched posture, and dehydration, although some gerbils have no obvious signs before death. Sudden death or death after a short period of illness is often indicative of this disease.

If one of your gerbils exhibits the symptoms of this disease, immediately separate the sick gerbil from the healthy ones. Place him in a covered carrying cage and take him to your veterinarian. Treatment with the appropriate antibiotics can sometimes save the sick gerbil. If your veterinarian suspects Tyzzer's disease, antibiotics will be provided for both (or all) of your pets. Accurate diagnosis of Tyzzer's disease can only be made by a veterinary pathologist's examination of a dead animal.

Poor husbandry and stress are implicated in this disease. Gerbils appear most susceptible following weaning, shipping, and adjustment to a new environment. Prevention is easier than treatment. Fortunately, this disease is rare in well-cared-for gerbils.

Noninfectious Diseases

Noninfectious diseases and other ailments are caused by common, everyday factors. They are not usually life-threatening ailments,

FAMILY-FRIENDLY TIP

Zoonotic Diseases

Parents are often concerned as to whether gerbils can give their children an illness, especially because children often forget to wash their hands after playing with their pets. Zoonotic diseases, such as salmonella and tapeworms, can be transmitted from animals to people. However, compared to all other types of small pets, gerbils present few potential health hazards to humans. These diseases have rarely been reported in colonies of gerbils. Your veterinarian will be aware of zoonotic diseases and can help you take preventative measures if your pet is diagnosed with such an illness. The potential for disease transmission is reduced with proper hygiene, such as washing your hands after playing with your pets and keeping their cage clean. Purchasing your gerbils from a clean environment rather than a smelly, dirty one further reduces the chance of a gerbil having a zoonotic disease.

but they still should be evaluated and treated by a veterinarian. Some common gerbil ailments are discussed in this section.

Ear Ailments

If your gerbil holds his head at an angle, he might have a benign ear cyst called a cholesteatoma. There is currently no treatment for this condition. Luckily, affected gerbils seem to adapt and can still live long lives. If your gerbil walks in circles, he probably has an infection of the inner ear. The inner ear is involved in balance, which is why your pet becomes disoriented and unbalanced. You might notice that he is also less active and has a poor appetite. An inner ear infection is potentially serious and is likely painful for your pet. Such symptoms warrant an immediate trip to the vet, who will prescribe an antibiotic as part of the treatment.

Kidney Disease

Older gerbils, those between 2 ½ and 4 years, sometimes get kidney disease. Typical symptoms are weight loss, poor appetite, and lethargy. If you notice these symptoms, along with an increase in water consumption, your gerbil might have kidney disease. Unfortunately, there is no treatment for this condition. As always, minimizing any stress can be helpful.

Lumps and Bumps

Tumors, which are a form of cancer, are a noninfectious disease. They are seldom seen in young gerbils. More often, tumors occur in middle-aged (two years of age) and older gerbils. When playing with your pet, you might notice a swelling under the skin, which could be a tumor or abscess. If you find a lump, consult a veterinarian to determine whether it is a tumor and whether surgery is needed.

One of the most common locations for tumors is the scent gland on a gerbil's

Proper husbandry is the best way to ensure good health.

Prevention

When properly cared for, gerbils are less stressed and have better natural resistance to diseases. Good food and a clean cage are some of the most important ways that you can help your gerbils stay healthy. Spoiled food and a dirty cage are invitations to illness. Routine hygiene is the most effective way to prevent disease organisms from becoming established in the enclosure and overpowering your gerbils' natural resistance to disease. Your gerbils are most likely to get sick when you become forgetful about cleaning their cage.

Pay attention to your gerbils' physical health and behavior. Note any weight changes and feel for lumps and bumps. Significant changes in the amount of food or water consumed and in activity and behavior are also important to note and could signal illness. Knowing a gerbil's regular behavior is helpful for detecting when he is not feeling well.

belly. Both males and females have a large scent gland in the middle of their belly that is used for marking territory. This normal gland is sometimes mistaken for a tumor. However, in older gerbils, especially males, the gland may

become infected or cancerous. A tumor might start as a small pimple-like growth. If the tumor continues to grow, it can bleed and become infected. If you notice any changes in the size or shape of this gland, take your gerbil to the veterinarian for an examination. Whenever possible, immediate surgical removal is best.

Malocclusion of the Teeth

Like all rodents, gerbils have chisel-like incisors in the front of their mouths. These teeth never stop growing. The incisor teeth enable them to carry nuts and other food items and to easily

Sometimes gerbils can be accidentally injured in a fall.

open hard seeds and nuts. The incisors are worn down by gnawing and chewing on hard substances. Although not common, the teeth of some gerbils need veterinary attention because of malocclusion. This condition occurs when the incisor teeth do not meet properly, either because they are overgrown or because they are misaligned. A gerbil's teeth can fail to meet and wear properly for several reasons. Malocclusion can be inherited, or it can be caused by trauma, such as loss of an incisor, infection, or improper diet. (For example, the gerbil does not regularly eat foods that are hard enough to wear down his teeth.) Even if you inspected your gerbil's teeth before buying him, be aware that hereditary malocclusion is often not detectable in young gerbils. Even if the teeth appear normal at first, as the animal grows, his teeth may become misaligned.

Gerbils with this condition eventually cannot eat, rapidly lose weight, and die without treatment. Some show symptoms often referred to as "slobbers," which are threads of saliva around the mouth and sometimes wiped on the front paws. If you notice that your pet is not eating, check his incisors by pulling back his lips. An affected gerbil should be taken to a veterinarian, who will clip or file his teeth.

Red Tears

Moist or dried red tears on the fur around a gerbil's eyes are not caused by blood. The red color is due to fluid secreted by the Harderian gland, which is located behind the eyes. The gland secretes fluid that keeps the eye moist and performs other functions. The fluid then drains into the outer part of a gerbil's nose through the nasolacrimal duct. Sometimes, gerbils also will have red tears around their nose. It is thought that this condition is caused by stress, an inadequate diet, or a dirty cage. It even may occur in conjunction with another illness. Monitor your gerbil's condition, and if he does not get better, take him to the vet.

Your gerbils are dependent on you to provide them with the proper environment.

Seizures

Experts estimate that between 20 and 40 percent of gerbils develop seizures when they are about two months of age. This condition is inherited and is seen in certain selectively bred lines. The seizures are usually over in a few minutes and have no long-term effects. During a seizure, the gerbil suddenly appears rigid and usually lies motionless or trembling on the cage floor. Some gerbils have more severe attacks with jerking, erratic movements before collapsing. If your gerbil has a seizure while you have him out of his cage, return him to his home until he recovers.

Many gerbils outgrow this condition, and it does not seem to affect life expectancy. The seizures may occur when a gerbil is exposed to a new environment, is frightened, or is not used to being handled. There is no treatment for seizures, although minimizing stress can reduce their frequency. Unfortunately, it is not known whether animals purchased at a pet store are susceptible to seizures. Hobbyists can decrease the incidence of this ailment by not breeding those gerbils who have seizures. This approach has already begun to reduce the incidence of seizures in these pets.

Strokes

Paralysis on one side of the body or dragging the hind limbs has been attributed to strokes. No treatment is available for a gerbil who has had a stroke. The symptoms usually disappear within a week, but some gerbils have a persistent limp that does not go away. Until your pet is able to move more naturally, keep his food and water in an easily accessed location near his nest box. If he does not recover and is unable to eat and drink, it is best to take him to the vet to have him painlessly put to sleep.

Improper Husbandry

When properly cared for, gerbils are less stressed and have better natural

resistance to diseases. However, a plethora of problems can affect gerbils because of poor husbandry. "Husbandry" is a big word that describes how a pet is taken care of and includes aspects such as housing, food, and water. Your gerbils are completely dependent on you to provide them with the proper environment. They cannot modify the size, temperature, air circulation, and cleanliness of their home. Providing good food and a clean cage are some of the most important ways that you can help your gerbils stay healthy; spoiled food and a dirty cage are invitations for illness. Routine cleaning is the most effective method to prevent disease organisms from becoming established in your gerbils' home and overpowering their natural resistance to disease. Your pets are most likely to get sick when you become forgetful about cleaning their environment.

Senior Gerbils

As a gerbil gets older, you might begin to notice changes in his behavior and body condition due to aging. Symptoms often appear so gradually in old animals that pet owners do not notice. However, middle-aged and older gerbils are more prone to illnesses than when they were young. Noninfectious ailments such as tumors are usually seen in older animals. Seniors also have a tendency to gain weight and to groom themselves less frequently; as a result, their fur no longer looks as sleek and shiny.

Chapter 6

Being Good

The fun part about owning gerbils is having them eat out of your hands and taking them out of their cage to play. Taming your pets will help you win their confidence and become their trusted friend.

Taming

A tame gerbil will let you hold him and pick him up without becoming frightened. The more time you spend holding and playing with a gerbil, the more quickly he will learn to trust you and become tame. If a gerbil is sleeping when you want to play with him, call his name, tap on his nest box, and allow him a few moments to wake up before you visit. Forcing him to come out when he would clearly rather sleep is not a good way to start taming a pet. Often the best time to visit is when he is already awake and playing. Establishing a routine, such as visiting at the same time each evening, can help with the taming process.

Gerbils can be wiggly and active, so it is usually best to start taming them by keeping your hand inside their cage, rather than taking the animals out. Let each gerbil sniff and crawl on your hand. (They need to have time to get used to your smell and the sound of your voice.) Place a food treat in the palm of your hand and encourage the gerbil to climb onto it. His curiosity will prompt him to investigate and eat the treat. Do not startle him by making sudden movements or loud noises. If the gerbil seems confident, slowly move your hand, and occasionally use a finger to pet him along his side, head, or tail. Even a brief stroke will work. Continue to slowly pet each gerbil in

the cage under a variety of conditions and at a variety of different times.

Eventually, your pets will hop into your hands. They might even climb out of the cage and up your arm. If you replace the gerbils in their home before they get too far up your arm, they will renew their quest to explore outside their cage with vigor and confidence. Once your gerbils are familiar with you and daily life in your home, household noise and events are unlikely to frighten them.

When you pass your gerbils' cage, call their names and say hello. Once your gerbils know you, they will run to the cage door to greet you, asking for attention. If you consistently work with your gerbils, they will soon trust you and want to spend time with you.

Depending on the gerbil, expect the taming process to take a few days to a week. However, some timid individuals might require more time and patience. Your gerbils are likely to become tame more quickly if you visit with them more than once a day. Use your pets' response to you to judge how fast to proceed. If a gerbil becomes skittish, go slower. Likewise, if your gerbils are bold and confident, you have done a good job. You can help to earn your gerbils' trust by remembering that the way to their heart is through their stomachs. Offering some food or a favorite treat in your fingers will help them learn to like you.

A tame gerbil will let you hold him and pick him up.

89

Being Good

Proper Handling

Pick up a gerbil by letting him climb onto your hand or by scooping him up under his belly. Gerbils can be frightened when a hand descends over their back, so always put your hand in the cage palm up, lower it to the bottom of the cage, and then move it toward the gerbil. Practice picking up each gerbil in the cage before taking them out. Gerbils do not like to be held for very long or to be restrained while being held. If you try to hold a gerbil securely in your hands, he probably will struggle and push through your fingers with his nose to try to get away. If you insist on restraining him, he may try to bite you out of fear.

Until a gerbil is familiar with you, it is sometimes necessary to use a container to scoop him up to take him out of his cage. Try using the cardboard roll from toilet paper or a tall yogurt or cottage cheese container. (Many gerbils especially seem to enjoy the dark, burrow-like cardboard roll.) Be sure to block both openings of the roll with your hands so that the gerbil won't accidentally leap out. Once your pet is tame, block only one end of the roll and pet him when he peeks his head out at the other end.

Gerbils do not like being scooped up in a plastic or glass container because the smooth sides do not let them hold onto anything. Scooping up some shavings from the cage along with a gerbil will make him less nervous when in a smooth, bare container. Be sure that the container you choose easily fits into and out of the cage. Do not chase him around the cage with the container. Place it on the cage floor near a corner and gently coax and herd him into it. You also can place a tasty treat inside the container to encourage your pet to willingly enter. Cover the top of the container with one hand to prevent your gerbil from leaping out. Talk reassuringly to him to help him learn that this procedure is nothing to fear.

Gerbils are nimble and will often try to get away, so hold the base of your pet's tail (not the tip!) with one hand and cradle his body in the palm of your other hand. Do not turn him over on his back and expose his belly. This posture makes gerbils (and most animals) feel vulnerable, and they will become upset and struggle frantically to right themselves. Keep in mind that a normally docile gerbil might bite you when he is in pain or frightened.

Gerbils do not like being held for very long.

Some gerbils can be taught simple tricks such as sitting up on their hind legs for a treat or navigating through a homemade maze to get a treat. All tricks rely on a small piece of tasty food as a reward. Gerbils are not generally as smart as other small pets such as rats, rabbits, and ferrets. It is easiest to train a behavior that a gerbil would normally do anyway, such as standing up on his hind legs, which he does to smell something interesting.

When training your gerbil, start by rewarding him for exhibiting the behavior for a short period of time. Suppose you want to teach him to stand and walk a few steps on his hind legs. You begin by rewarding your gerbil when he merely stands up on his hind legs. Hold the food reward where your gerbil can see or smell it when he is on all four legs, and then move the reward above his head so that he stands up to get it.

You also can say "up" to your gerbil at the same time. Eventually, require your gerbil to stay on his hind legs for longer periods of time before you reward him. Continue this method by moving the reward a little in front of him so that he has to walk to reach the reward. You can gradually extend the distance he has to walk on his hind legs until he has taken a few steps.

This type of training is called the method of approximation, or shaping. You shape your gerbil's behavior by rewarding those behaviors that are close to the behavior that you want. As you train, have your gerbil do a little more each time until he is doing exactly what you want. Use a food reward to reinforce his behavior. The food must be very tasty, and you must use only a very small piece or your gerbil will quickly fill up and lose interest in the training.

You can become your gerbil's playground!

Even after a gerbil is calm and tame, it is sometimes best to use two hands to hold him. Loud noises and sudden movements, your own or those caused by another person or pet, could scare him and cause him to jump out of your hand. For this reason, one hand should support your gerbil's body while your other hand is cupped over his back. Snuggle your gerbil against your body for greater security. It also is prudent to immediately sit on the ground when first teaching a gerbil to be held. Then, if he does jump, the distance is much less than if you were standing.

Don't pick a gerbil up by his tail. For one thing, he can turn and bite your finger, which will probably cause you to drop him. For another thing, the skin on the gerbil's tail will come off. The tail will eventually atrophy and fall off, or a veterinarian will need to amputate it. A gerbil can live without his tail,

but careful handling on your part will prevent tail loss from ever happening.

Veterinarians will sometimes pick up a gerbil using the loose skin on the back of his neck. Doing so reduces a gerbil's struggles and allows the veterinarian to easily examine him. However, there's really no reason for you to use this method. Unless you pick up your gerbil by his skin just right, he can rotate around and bite you.

Gerbil Body Language

Knowing your gerbils' body language can help you to be more sensitive to their moods, which will help you to tame them better.

Do not continue playing with your gerbils if they become scared. When nervous, gerbils sit stiffly with their front paws held tightly in front of their chest, or they rapidly wash their face. As part of the "flight or fight response," some frightened gerbils defecate. When frightened, your pet also might flatten himself close to the ground, run away, or bite. If your pet engages in any of these behaviors, talk gently to him and then put him back into his house so that he can calm down.

Some gerbils bounce about their cage when they are happy. You also might hear your pets' softly grinding their teeth together when they are content.

When curious, gerbils will stand up on their hind legs, with ears alert and noses twitching, to investigate their surroundings.

Preventing Fights
Within family groups and pairs, there is always a dominance hierarchy. Usually a larger gerbil is dominant over a smaller gerbil. A submissive gerbil will try to appease the dominant gerbil by licking the dominant gerbil's mouth or

rubbing his back on the belly gland of the dominant animal.

When playing and fighting, gerbils often push at each other with their front paws. When they are angry and ready to fight, they lay their ears back, lash their tails back and forth, and box with their front paws. In addition, you may hear your pets grind their teeth together. If one gerbil does not flee, they will soon latch onto each other, rolling about as they fight. Fights among gerbils can be vicious, with the combatants inflicting serious bite wounds on each other. In some cases, fights can even lead to the death of one gerbil if he cannot escape his foe. If you are around when your gerbils begin to fight, use gloves or a towel to separate them. Never use your hands because you are likely to be accidentally bitten.

Playtime
Gerbils are fun to watch while they play in their cage. However, part of the

Household Hazards

When your gerbils are allowed playtime outside their cage, you must protect them from certain household hazards. Some hazards can even prove fatal to them. Here are a few common dangers:

- appliances
- crushing injuries from doors, or being sat or stepped on
- electrical cords
- household chemicals
- open doors and windows
- sticky traps, snap traps, rodent poisons
- toilets
- wastebaskets

books. Close up nooks and crannies so that your gerbils do not escape. Place your pets' cage on the floor and let them begin their exploration.

Your pets' cage is their refuge, and it gives them a sense of security and safety. Should your gerbils become scared, they can quickly run back into their cage. If your gerbils live in an aquarium, use a bird ladder to allow them easy access in and out of the cage.

Always Watch Your Pets

Never let your pets loose in a room without supervising them. Watch them closely so that they do not chew items or become "lost" by finding a secret cubbyhole for a new sleeping

fun of owning gerbils is taking them out of their cage to play. The more you play with your pets, the happier and friendlier they will be. You can make yourself into your pets' playground. Let them play on you while you sit on a bed or a chair and read a book or watch television. Your gerbils will scamper back and forth across your shoulders and burrow behind your hair. They'll crawl down your sleeves and explore your pockets. You can even teach your pets to ride on your shoulder for short periods of time.

Many people allow their pets to explore and play in the room in which the cage is kept. Before doing this, you must "gerbil-proof" the room. Pick up "edible" items off the floor. Gerbils can eat and dig up potted plants and can chew electrical cords, papers, and

Be sure to supervise out-of-cage playtime.

nest. Gerbils have little awareness of heights and will tumble off the edge of a bed, table, or chair, falling and potentially breaking a bone. Be aware that your gerbils might leave droppings in the room as they explore. (They cannot be housetrained.)

Going Back Into the Cage

If you want your pets to return to their cage but they still want to explore, do not chase after them. Doing so is sure to scare them and will prolong the time it takes to entice them back into their cage. Gerbils can run fast and may be difficult to catch. Most loose gerbils, however, will explore a room and will not hide. They will return to their cage or your hand if tempted by a treat. To encourage your pets to re-enter their home, try placing fresh-smelling fruit or vegetable treats in their food dish. Unlike pet rats, gerbils are not readily taught to come when called by name.

One way to teach your gerbils to return to their cage and to know where their cage is located in relation to the rest of the room is to only let them explore a small area around the enclosure each day. Always place their cage in the same location in the room in which they are allowed to play. When your gerbils pop up and are ready to leave the enclosure, put them back inside. They will bounce around and try to leave again. This time, let them get a little farther before you place them back in their cage. Over time, your gerbils will hop around trying different routes to get away from you, and in so doing,

Separation

Be aware that if your pair of gerbils was temporarily separated for more than a day, you should slowly reintroduce them over a few days.

they will learn the area around their cage. Eventually, allow your gerbils to explore farther and farther away from it. By minimizing the initial distance in which they are allowed to play, gerbils develop a map of their cage and their exploration room. Gerbils can be bold and inquisitive. Nonetheless, by proceeding slowly, you can help them become confident that there is nothing frightening in their expanded environment.

Playpens

Other options for play outside your pets' cage include a bathroom tub, a large plastic enclosure made especially for small pets that you can set up much like a child's playpen, or a high-sided plastic swimming pool. Place nest boxes and toys in the playground. Make sure that any enclosure you use is escape-proof.

Other Household Pets

Do not expect your gerbils to get along with other pets that you may have, including other species of gerbil. Even a parrot with clipped wings might leave his perch and dive-bomb an exploring gerbil if given the chance. As long as they can escape, gerbils can survive an encounter with more placid herbivorous pets such as guinea pigs and hamsters, but an omnivorous pet rat will readily kill an unsupervised gerbil.

Ferrets, cats, and dogs are a gerbil's natural enemies. Your gerbils will not become friends with pets that are likely to kill and eat them. Gerbils are an ideal-sized prey for cats, and few felines can resist stalking and pouncing on a gerbil. Some gerbil owners with obedience-trained dogs have taught them to let their gerbils smell and walk on them.

Such dogs are unusual and typically have a low prey drive. Interestingly, gerbils often behave aggressively toward the dog at first, nipping his feet or nose if he is too pushy. But without any aggression from the dog, gerbils eventually treat him as a play toy to run over and investigate.

While your other family pets will not be friends with your gerbils, you must train them to leave your gerbils and their cage alone. Correct your dog if he barks, paws at the cage, jumps around, or otherwise scares your gerbils. Do not let your cat sit on or lie down next to your gerbils' cage. Boisterous dogs and persistent cats can knock over the cage, which is quite stressful and frightening for them. If necessary, your gerbils' home should be kept behind a closed door to protect them from other pets.

Run-About Balls

Large-sized plastic run-about balls designed for hamsters are a safe option for allowing your gerbils to exercise outside their cage. The minimum size to use for a gerbil is 7 inches (17.8 cm). Only one gerbil can be placed in a run-about ball at a time. Supervise your pets when they are in the run-about balls, because falling down stairs, getting stuck in place, and other pets are potential hazards. Your gerbil also might chew anything he can reach through the ventilation holes in the ball. If he stops on an electrical cord, he can chew it and possibly electrocute himself. Some balls are designed to move on a race track, which helps to confine a gerbil's movements to a safe place.

Compared to a cage, run-about balls have little ventilation, so do not keep your pet confined in one for more than a half hour at a time. When tired, a gerbil usually stops moving and sits

in the ball. These balls can be used outside on a smooth lawn, but gerbils do not like being so exposed, and much of their activity in the ball is due to fear. The hot sun also can cook your gerbil, so only use a run-about ball inside your home. Wash and dry the ball after each use.

If you have more than one pair of gerbils and keep them in separate cages, provide each pair with their own run-about ball. Some gerbils will become agitated and urinate and mark excessively when placed inside a ball that has been used by another unknown individual. Even if you wash the ball, a gerbil's keen sense of smell and territorial nature will stress him.

Introducing Gerbils to Each Other

What should you do if one of your gerbils dies and the remaining gerbil

is lonely? You should try to introduce a new gerbil. However, you cannot just place a new gerbil into your pet's cage and expect all to be well. Gerbils are territorial and will not accept an unfamiliar gerbil. Adult gerbils placed together in a cage for the first time will fight, often to the death.

Cages that you use for the introduction should be new, which is an unanticipated cost. Your original gerbil will resent any newcomer's intrusion into his territory. He will be very aggressive in defending it, and the success of pairing him with a new gerbil will be reduced.

Choose a younger gerbil between five to eight weeks old to increase the chances for success. Younger gerbils tend to be more readily accepted than another adult.

Several methods can be used to facilitate the introduction. Place your original gerbil in a wire cage, and place the new gerbil in another wire cage. Slide the two cages together so that the gerbils can smell each other through the cage bars. Alternatively, you can try dividing a wire cage or aquarium with a piece of stiff, heavy gauge wire mesh with spaces less than ¼ inch (0.64 cm). Securely place the wire so that the weight of a gerbil pressing against it will not cause the mesh to fall or allow a gerbil to crawl under or around it. If the mesh gives way, the gerbils could reach each other and they will fight. The spaces between the wire mesh also should be small enough that a gerbil cannot push his nose through and bite the other gerbil, especially on the toes of his front paws. Another method to try is to place a smaller cage inside a larger cage. Tuck the small cage in a corner so that only two sides of the enclosure are exposed to the

Slowly introduce new gerbils to each other.

gerbil living in the larger cage.

Over the next several days, switch the gerbils and handfuls of bedding from their cages several times a day between the cages or sides of the cage. Usually the two gerbils will accept each other within several days. If they fight, you must continue switching them back and forth for several more days before once again housing them within the same cage. Carefully watch your gerbils for the first few days that they share a home to make sure that they do not fight and have accepted one another. Any wounds from bites could indicate that the two gerbils still do not like each other.

Females are more likely to be aggressive to a strange gerbil than are male gerbils. Males in particular can be much more accepting of a very young gerbil. If you add a young gerbil to an older gerbil, you eventually will face the same problem of a gerbil without a partner. Consider adding a pair of younger gerbils about five weeks old. Then, when the older gerbil dies, the two remaining gerbils

Taming your pets will help you win their confidence and become their trusted friend.

will have approximately the same life span. Follow the same method of introduction as you would with a single gerbil.

If you cannot add another gerbil, be sure to give your single gerbil plenty of attention and exercise.

Quarantine

One caution about introducing a new gerbil to your current pet is the potential risk of also introducing an illness. Serious hobbyists who breed gerbils usually quarantine a new arrival from their other gerbils, even if the newcomer seems healthy. A quarantine period helps to prevent the transmission of illness among gerbils. The new arrival is kept in a cage as far away as possible from the other animals.

The quarantine period can last from two to three weeks. During this time, the gerbil's health is monitored. When the isolation period ends, the newcomer can be moved into the area containing the other gerbils, assuming he has exhibited no signs of ill health. Although pet owners rarely quarantine a new arrival, often because it means having to buy another cage and

accessories, the best approach is always to quarantine a new arrival. However, if you purchased your new gerbil from a serious breeder or a clean pet store, there is probably a low risk of any illness. Nonetheless, it is still a stressful time for both gerbils, and stress can cause gerbils to become sick.

Problem Behaviors

Gerbils do not have many problem behaviors. However, a few of the most common are described in this section.

Nipping

If your pets are housed in a wire cage, do not feed them through the cage bars. Otherwise, anything (including a finger) that is poked through the cage might get nipped. Always open the cage door to offer a treat. In addition, wash your hands before handling your gerbils in case any food scents on your hands entice them to nip.

Biting

Gerbils are even-tempered and not easily provoked to bite. However, if they feel threatened or frightened, they might stamp their hind leg as a sign that they will bite if you do not stop your threatening behavior. If your gerbil does bite you, say "No" and try blowing on his face to discourage the behavior. If one or both of your newly acquired gerbils bites and none of your taming efforts seem to work, consider returning your pet(s) to the place of purchase. This type of nasty temperament might be hereditary and cannot be cured.

Problems With Pairs

Sometimes a pair of gerbils that have been housed together for a long time might suddenly begin to fight. It's also possible that you never noticed the dynamic between the gerbils. If one of your gerbils is constantly chased, squeaks excessively, or hides by himself while the other gerbil is out eating or playing, there could be a problem. Check to see if the timid gerbil has scabs, bites, or chewed fur, especially near his rump, which is a sign that he has been bitten by the other gerbil. If the gerbils continue to fight, keep them in two separate cages.

Digging

Gerbils often develop stereotypical digging behavior that begins when they are about 30 days old. A gerbil will dig vigorously and repeatedly in the bedding in the corners of the cage. Pet owners often think that their gerbil is trying to escape, but the digging is caused by his natural instinct to burrow. Providing a gerbil with an L-shaped burrow can reduce this behavior. Scientists have found that stereotypical digging will not develop in gerbils if they receive an artificial L-shaped burrow before they are a month old. The artificial burrow can be made of dark, hard plastic. Check the plumbing-supply section at a hardware store for pipes that can be used in your pets' cage. Try to connect the burrow to your pets' nest box to more accurately replicate their natural burrow.

Resources

Gerbils

Clubs and Societies

The American Gerbil Society, Inc. (AGS)
PO Box 1687
New York, NY 10159-1687
www.agsgerbils.org

South West and Midland Gerbil Club (UK)
Show secretary: Annmarie Hey
3 Fairhaven
Yate Bristol, South Gloucestershire
BS37 4DS England
www.pyrpport.com/swmgc
Email: SWMGC@pyroport.com

Internet Resources

The following websites contain information on all aspects of gerbil care and links to other informative websites.

Animal Hospitals, USA
www.animalhospitals-usa.com/small_pets/gerbils.html
Animal Hospitals USA offers healthcare information for treating sick or injured dogs, cats, birds, guinea pigs, gerbils, ferrets, prairie dogs, and reptiles. As veterinarians and devoted animal caregivers, our supporting animal hospitals and clinics are committed to giving your pets the best medical care possible. Restoring your pet's health is our first and only mission.

Healthypet
www.healthypet.com
Healthypet.com is part of the American Animal Hospital Association, an organization of more than 29,000 veterinary care providers committed to providing excellence in small animal care.

The National Gerbil Society (UK)
www.gerbils.co.uk
The NGS pages provide information on the National Gerbil Society, gerbils, and how to keep them.

Petfinder
www.petfinder.org
Petfinder.org provides an extensive database of adoptable animals, shelters, and rescue groups around the country. You can also post classified ads for lost or found pets, pets wanted, and pets needing homes.

Pet Parade
www.pet-parade.com/gerbils
Breeder and pet care resources.

Petshub
http://petshub.com/gerbils
Pet care information and resources.

Pets911
www.1888pets911.org
Pets 911 offers a comprehensive database of lost and found pets, adoption information, pet health, and shelter and rescue information. The website also runs a toll-free phone hotline (1-888-PETS-911) that gives pet owners access to important life-saving information.

VetQuest
www.vin.com/vetquest/index0.html
VetQuest is an online veterinary search
and referral service. You can search its
database for over 25,000 veterinary
hospitals and clinics all over the world.
The service places special emphasis
on veterinarians with advanced
online access to the latest health
care information and highly qualified
veterinary specialists and consultants.

Rescue and Adoption Organizations

**American Society for the Prevention of
Cruelty to Animals**
424 East 92nd Street
New York, NY 10128-6801
Telephone: (212) 876-7700
www.aspca.org
information@aspca.org

American Humane Association (AHA)
63 Inverness Drive East
Englewood, CO 80112
Telephone: (303) 792-9900
Fax: 792-5333
www.americanhumane.org

**Humane Society of the United States
(HSUS)**
2100 L Street, NW
Washington, DC 20037
Telephone: (202)- 452-1100
www.hsus.org

**Royal Society for the Prevention of
Cruelty to Animals (RSPCA)**
Telephone: 0870 3335 999
Fax: 0870 7530 284
www.rspca.org.uk

Emergency Services

**ASPCA National Animal Poison Control
Center**
Telephone: 1-888-426-4435
www.aspca.org

Animal Poison Hotline
Telephone: (888) 232-8870

Veterinary and Health Resources

**Academy of Veterinary Homeopathy
(AVH)**
P.O. Box 9280
Wilmington, DE 19809
Telephone: (866) 652-1590
Fax: (866) 652-1590
E-mail: office@TheAVH.org
www.theavh.org

**American Academy of Veterinary
Acupuncture (AAVA)**
100 Roscommon Drive, Suite 320
Middletown, CT 06457
Telephone: (860) 635-6300
Fax: (860) 635-6400
E-mail: office@aava.org
www.aava.org

**American Animal Hospital Association
(AAHA)**
P.O. Box 150899
Denver, CO 80215-0899
Telephone: (303) 986-2800
Fax: (303) 986-1700
E-mail: info@aahanet.org
www.aahanet.org/index.cfm

American College of Veterinary Internal Medicine (ACVIM)
1997 Wadsworth Blvd., Suite A
Lakewood, CO 80214-5293
Telephone: (800) 245-9081
Fax: (303) 231-0880
Email: ACVIM@ACVIM.org
www.acvim.org

American College of Veterinary Ophthalmologists (ACVO)
P.O. Box 1311
Meridian, Idaho 83860
Telephone: (208) 466-7624
Fax: (208) 466-7693
E-mail: office@acvo.com
www.acvo.com

American Holistic Veterinary Medical Association (AHVMA)
2218 Old Emmorton Road
Bel Air, MD 21015
Telephone: (410) 569-0795
Fax: (410) 569-2346
E-mail: office@ahvma.org
www.ahvma.org

Gerbils

American Veterinary Chiropractic Association (AVCA)
442154 E 140 Rd.
Bluejacket, OK 74333
Telephone: (918) 784-2231
E-mail: amvetchiro@aol.com
www.animalchiropractic.org

American Veterinary Medical Association (AVMA)
1931 North Meacham Road – Suite 100
Schaumburg, IL 60173
Telephone: (847) 925-8070
Fax: (847) 925-1329
E-mail: avmainfo@avma.org
www.avma.org

Animal Behavior Society
Indiana University
2611 East 10th Street #170
Bloomington IN 47408-2603
Telephone: (812) 856-5541
E-mail: aboffice@indiana.edu
www.animalbehavior.org

ASPCA Animal Poison Control Center
1717 South Philo Road, Suite 36
Urbana, IL 61802
Telephone: (888) 426-4435
www.aspca.org

British Veterinary Association (BVA)
7 Mansfield Street
London
W1G 9NQ
Telephone: 020 7636 6541
Fax: 020 7436 2970
E-mail: bvahq@bva.co.uk
www.bva.co.uk

Orthopedic Foundation for Animals (OFA)
2300 NE Nifong Blvd
Columbus, Missouri 65201-3856
Telephone: (573) 442-0418
Fax: (573) 875-5073
Email: ofa@offa.org
www.offa.org

Publications

Magazines

Critters USA
Fancy Publications, Inc.
3 Burroughs
Irvine, CA 92618
Telephone: (888) 738-2665
www.fancypubs.com

Books

Fox, Sue, *The Quick & Easy Guide to Gerbil Care*, TFH Publications, Inc.

Fox, Sue, *The Guide to Owning a Gerbil*, TFH Publications, Inc.

Kotter, Engelbert, *Gerbils*, Barron's.

Sino, Betsy Sikora, *The Gerbil: An Owner's Guide to a Happy Healthy Pet*, Howell Book House.

Viner, Bradley, *All About Your Gerbil*, Barron's.

Index

Note: Boldfaced numbers indicate illustrations.

Gerbils

Gerbils

About the Author

Sue Fox is the author of numerous books on small animals and several breeds of dog. Her home in the Sierra Nevada Mountains of California is shared with a happy menagerie.

Photo Credits